A THOUSAND MORNINGS OF MUSIC

also by Arnold Gingrich

BUSINESS & THE ARTS: AN ANSWER TO TOMORROW   1969
TOYS OF A LIFETIME   1966
AMERICAN TROUT FISHING
  by Theodore Gordon and a Company of Anglers (edited)   *1966*
THE WELL-TEMPERED ANGLER   1965
THE PAT HOBBY STORIES
  by F. Scott Fitzgerald (edited)   *1962*
CAST DOWN THE LAUREL   1935

Arnold Gingrich

A Thousand Mornings of Music

of
Music

THE
JOURNAL
OF AN
OBSESSION
WITH THE
VIOLIN

CROWN PUBLISHERS, INC.
NEW YORK

To Lee Wurlitzer Roth

ACKNOWLEDGMENTS

I am greatly indebted to Henry Wolf for the main body of this book's photographs as well as for its jacket design; to Marianne Wurlitzer Bruck, for the gatherings of photographs and models of instruments for the appendices, and for important photographic embellishments of its main text; to William and Wilda Moennig, and to Mrs. Luthier Rosenthal and her son, David, for essential photographs at appropriate points in the narrative; to Dario d'Attili, for saving me from several errors of fact while leaving me free rein to make what may well be even more numerous errors of opinion; to Simone Fernando Sacconi, for his welcome photograph of Fritz Kreisler; to Jane Kendall Gingrich, for the childhood photograph of Rafael Druian; to Rafael Druian, himself, for guidance over the entire three years of the volume's inception and, after its completion, for finally breaking me of fifty years' dependence on that beginner's crutch, the use of a shoulder pad; to Hermann Kessler, for getting up at dawn to provide what would otherwise have been missing links in the photographic documentation; to both my amanuenses, Anne Fuchs Cazeneuve and Jed McGarvey, for assists beyond the customary norm; to Louise Stern, for invaluable research and production assistance; to Bayard Schieffelin and John Miller of the New York Public Library for the indispensable boon of *denkensraum;* to my teachers, Harry Shub and Marjorie Garrigue Mendel, for vastly increasing my already towering respect for the instrument; to Joseph Eger, of the New York Orchestral Society, for services as *deus ex machina* in arranging the climactic event; and above all to Lee Wurlitzer Roth and Charles Ponall, for the circumstances that led them, quite apart from any conscious intent, to lend the whole story its point.

TABLE OF CONTENTS

Acknowledgments   vii

A Thousand Mornings of Music   13

Appendices

  I   The Anatomy of a Violin: The 30 Locations of
     a Violin's 92 or 93 Parts   201

  II The Changing Standings of the Four Schools:
     The Relative Values of Stainer, Amati, Stradivari,
     and Guarneri Instruments in 1700, 1800, 1900,
     and Today   204

 III Some of the Violins Mentioned: A Gallery of the
     Famous Instruments from the Vaults at Rembert
     Wurlitzer, Inc.   209

 IV A List of Pertinent Addresses for Those Inter-
     ested in Playing or Collecting Fiddles   236

  V Inside the Shop: Workroom Scenes and Rec-
     ords, Including "The Fever Chart of a Violin"   245

 VI Genealogies: Charts Showing the Violin-making
     Members of the Four Families   250

A Selective Bibliography:
     Books Quoted, Mentioned, or Otherwise of
     Interest   253

A THOUSAND MORNINGS OF MUSIC

ONE

rnest Hemingway always said that the way to get rid of a thing was to write about it. For him that may well have been true, as on three occasions there was a new woman in his life, and each time it was right after he had written a novel celebrating her predecessor.

But what obviously worked for him one way seems to have worked for me, on at least one occasion, precisely in reverse.

In 1965, in the course of writing a book of memoirs couched in terms of the toys of my life—things I had once been obsessed by, and then laid away, as one does with toys, I devoted a part of one chapter to a farewell to the violin. The chapter was called "Simple Confession," in honor of one of the first tunes I had learned to play on the fiddle as a child, and I suppose one subconscious reason for calling it that was that it was a title I could never recall or encounter without a twinge of embarrassment.

I had played that piece "by heart," to my mother's accompaniment on the piano, at some small afternoon function, probably the meeting of a sewing circle or some similar group to which my mother belonged, and although I had got through it without any obvious mistake, I made what I felt ever after was a very silly error of speech, when one of the women undertook to congratulate me on my performance. She said something polite, to the effect that it had been "very nice," and to my immediate chagrin I found that what I had said, in a too hasty response to the compliment, was,

"I'm glad you appreciated it."

What a pompous remark that must have seemed, as if the little bagatelle I had played had been an esoteric masterwork! I could have bit my tongue for saying it, but my mortification over having it come out "appreciated," when all I really meant was "enjoyed," was so intense that by the time I rallied enough to attempt to correct it, she had turned away and was talking to another grownup and I didn't think it was appropriate for a ten-year-old to try to interrupt, especially at the risk of making another *gaffe* that might be worse than the first.

So I just brooded about it instead, for the next half century and more, quite evidently, because I still feel uncomfortable about it.

The chapter in question was devoted to the various losing battles in my lifelong war with the inanimate, and the gesture of ending it by "hanging up my fiddle and my bow" was meant as a token of abject and final surrender. But I must have made it with my fingers crossed, however unwittingly, because, as it turned out, nothing ever revivified my interest in the violin, which I had allowed to go untouched for as long as a year or so at a time over the better part of the preceding fifty years, so much as this act of bidding it goodbye.

My "giving up my music" would have occasioned no perceptible diminution of the gaiety of nations in any case, even if it had been for real, because I had long since reconciled myself to the realization that my standing, in relation to that most sensitive and exigent of instruments, was little more than that of a permanent beginner.

I had first taken it up with high resolve, intensified by relief at getting away from the piano, which I had detested for three years, and had indeed slaved away at it for a seven-year sentence of hard labor, largely self-imposed. I persisted at its pursuit long after parents, friends, and teachers had urged me, with remarkable unanimity, to give it up, but I realized by the age of fifteen that my undying love for it was going to go unrequited.

I had always had a romantic regard for the violin, going very nearly as far back as my memory goes. I spent my summers with my mother in Canada every year until I was ten, and one of the summers, either my seventh or my eighth, was the time when I first fell in love with a fiddle.

My mother had a niece who was only a couple of years younger than she was, whom I always called either Aunt Gertie or Auntie Gert, although she was my cousin, and she had a suitor that summer named Art Harris, who played the violin.

Art Harris obviously never set the world aflame, either with his fiddle or by any other means, or his name, even all these years later, would seem in some way familiar. One of my mother's suitors, for instance, was a young man named Noah Brousseau, and I don't expect that name to mean anything to you either, but when I tell you that he not long after won fame and fortune under the name of Tommy Burns, I anticipate more reaction. No, not now, perhaps, but for a few years before 1915, when he lost to Jess Willard, his was a name that was universally known, at least to small boys, as the heavyweight champion of the world.

So one of the two great misfortunes of my otherwise happy childhood, I felt for at least the greater part of its duration, was that my mother had picked the wrong husband, and the other was that so had Auntie Gert.

If it had been to me, and not to her, that Art Harris had been playing, that wonderful summer of 1910 or 1911, whichever it was, he'd have won me for life. But I was not the great prize he was after, nor was he himself any prize, apparently, compared at least to the man who had cut him out of her affections by the next summer. That was the man she married. The son of a department-store owner, he was much more obviously a gentleman than poor Art Harris. His name was W. A. G. Smythe, which gives you an idea, and it seemed to impress my Aunt Gertie too, despite my repeatedly pointing out that all that fancy name boiled down to, really, was Willie Smith.

This was enough to line me up forever on the side of Art, as against Commerce, and for many years I mourned the loss of Art Harris, gone out of my life after that one summer.

I can't remember now a single tune he played, though I suppose for the most part he played things like Schumann's *Traümerei* and Drdla's *Souvenir*. The showy pieces my mother played on the piano, like *The Death of Nelson* and *The Siege of Paris*, I'll remember forever, but of course I heard her play much more often than I heard Art Harris. But the two things I remember most vividly about his fiddling were the way he could make the instrument almost seem to sob, a thing that brought me frequently to the verge of tears, and the color of the violin itself, which was a wonderfully soft old yellow, just slightly rusty across the middle and around the edges. Since then I've undoubtedly heard many gypsy fiddlers, whose sobbings and moanings on the violin began where his left off, but not Kreisler himself ever impressed me later any more than Art Harris did then, and the remembered sight of his violin left me with a predilection for soft-hued old yellow fiddles that still endures.

At the time it gave me also the determination to get away from the piano, on which my mother had been giving me lessons from about the time I was six, and by my ninth birthday I had won my case, although Art Harris had lost his.

In the long run I was to lose mine too, or rather it was to prove to be a case not really worth having won. After giving up lessons at fifteen, and after an abortive attempt to make a violin had convinced me that I was even less gifted for making them than I was for playing them, I came to the conclusion that the fiddle and I, however starry-eyed I had once been about our future together, would have to become resigned to going through life as no more than just friends.

Not even close friends, either, for at least some sizable stretches of time. While I always kept a fiddle somewhere, strung up and ready to play, for years its accustomed place was the floor of a closet, and when I went away, whether for such short terms as summer camps or such longer ones as college semesters, it would never even occur to me to take it along, nor would I miss it enough to send for it.

Intense as my original infatuation with the instrument had been, I was far from the dedication of a Rembert Wurlitzer, for instance, who became a Princeton dropout and, before he was twenty, headed for Mirecourt and a year's apprenticeship in the craft of violin making. As a votary of the violin, he had the true vocation, and it must have been always evident, growing up as he did in a family with a mighty place in the music world, and surrounded since his cradle days with great instruments. His obsession with fiddles was lifelong, and its depth was evident in his letters home, which I have seen, written in 1924 and 1925. There could never have been any doubt that he would devote more of his time and his thoughts to the violin than would any other man of his time or indeed of the century that had elapsed since the days of Tarisio, the greatest violin hunter of all. But Rembert Wurlitzer combined livelihood with hobby, vocation with avocation, and occupation with preoccupation, to a degree that made his devotion to the instrument full time in a sense that was virtually unique. To compare my idle fiddle fancying to his would be fatuous to the point of absurdity. As soon compare my scrapings to the performance of a Paganini. No, my life with the violin soon became no more than a sometime thing, and I never even acquired a better instrument than my student one until the winter of 1936–1937, when my then

REMBERT WURLITZER IN 1925

Rembert Wurlitzer as a young luthier ca. 1925. He quit Princeton to pursue an atavistic urge to become a violin maker, studying a year in Mirecourt and in Italy. A violin made by him in 1925 was shown at the Loan Exhibition in New York in 1966.

Blackstone Studios

wife gave me an Aegidius Kloz, dated 1734, for my thirty-third birthday.

That came about because I had been using that instrument for some months, playing weekly duets with the wife of a colleague who lived down the street. It was her second fiddle, as indeed I was too, in the duets we played, which kept on most weeks for a matter of a couple of years, both before and after the violin became mine, until the colleague was one no longer, and the couple moved away.

The Kloz was mine for the next thirty years, and beyond the purchase of an occasional string and the not very frequent re-hairing of the Albert Nürnberger bow that went with it, I made no investment of money, and not much more of time, in the pursuit of happiness with a violin.

There seemed no point in having a better violin, since the Kloz, while no masterpiece even by that Mittenwald family's not-too-exalted standards, was still so much better than I was, or indeed could ever hope to become, given the very obvious limitations imposed by my long practice-proved lack of talent.

All this was true, and had been true, and doubtless would have remained so, if only I hadn't set it down in print, by way of saying a farewell to the violin, and dismissing my onetime obses-sion with it as an aberration of my youth. But then something strange happened. Almost as if it were because I said it was so, suddenly it was so no longer.

It was as if the obsession I had thought to exorcise by the process of "writing it out" had been aroused by the very procedure, and, stung by the incantation, had determined to possess me all over again, but this time for good.

The first intimation of it was in November of 1965, a matter of days after my fishing book, *The Well-Tempered Angler*, had been published. One of the first fan letters I got was from a fiddler, Rafael Druian, whom I had first met in Minneapolis in

1958 when he was concertmaster of the symphony there under Dorati, and had met again a couple of times afterward in Cleveland, where he had since become the concertmaster under Szell. Druian wrote me expressing surprise that in the number of times we had met neither of us had apparently ever suspected that the other fished. He wanted us to come to the next concert of the Cleveland Orchestra at Carnegie Hall, in February, and hoped that we would then get some chance to talk fishing. My wife Janie had known him in her Havana days in the twenties and thirties, when she was married to Grant Mason, and Rafael Druian had been sent from there, as a boy prodigy, to study at the Curtis Institute in Philadelphia. So I talked to her about coming in for the concert, and answered the letter confirming the date.

Hearing from a fiddler made me turn to look again at the chapter in *Toys of a Lifetime* devoted in large part to my war with the violin. The book was in the finished manuscript stage but not yet in proof, and, reading it over again for the first time after a lapse of some months since writing it, I began to wonder whether I had not exaggerated a little too much in telling about how bad I had been on the violin. I remembered that in my first book, thirty years before, I had advanced for myself on the dust jacket the rather tall claim that I was the world's worst fiddler, and was struck by the belated suspicion that perhaps I had said that just to make myself sound more interesting.

So I got out the Kloz, which I hadn't touched for months, and maybe not even for as much as a year, and rationalized to myself that in doing so I was "just testing."

To my surprise, I found that I could remember all four movements of the Handel E Major Sonata, Number Six, which I thought I had remembered working on for years as a kid and never managing to flounder through more than half to two-thirds of the way. I noticed that I was even playing it with some semblance of a vibrato, something I had not recalled ever suspecting myself of possessing.

I didn't for a minute think that my performance of this old bête

RAFAEL DRUIAN IN 1932

noire of my youth was any good, but I was nevertheless astonished that after a lapse of so many years I could remember all the notes, and that I could thus give it any sort of performance at all. I was, in fact, so amazed to think I could remember that many notes after that many years that, a few days later, feeling sure that it must have been a fluke, I tried it again, and found not only that I could still go all the way through it, but that it seemed a little easier to get through than it had the time before. This was interesting enough to warrant repetition, and I soon found that I was picking up the Kloz at decreasing intervals and spending hours with it, rather than minutes, each weekend.

One of those weekends, in late January of 1966, before the date that was to bring Rafael Druian to town along with the Cleveland Orchestra, I noticed something that I'd never happened to see in the Sunday *New York Times* before—an auction notice that included a lot of what purported to be old Italian violins. Seeing that the address was quite near my office, I tore it out of the paper and decided it wouldn't hurt to give those fiddles a look.

I found that they were old, but not very, being nineteenth-century fiddles. Four of them had labels, which the fifth lacked, and three of them bore the names of Italian makers, while the other was Irish. As for the unlabeled one, I thought it looked rather more German than Italian, as its lines were those of the Stainer model. According to the labels, one, which was dark red and pretty obviously a copy of the Grand Pattern Amati, was made by Felix Mori Costa in Parma in 1809; another, which was of orange and yellow and rather vaguely followed the Strad lines of the golden period, was made by Giuseppe Marconcini in Ferrara in 1822, and another, a clean yellow with the rather pointed Brescian or Gothic sound holes suggestive of the late Guarneri del Gesù model, was made by Antonio Guadagnini in Turin in 1851. The fourth bore the eccentrically worded label of John Delany of Dublin and was a nut-brown fiddle of no striking resemblance to any well-known maker's model and was chiefly interesting for the label's tag line, after the 1807 date, of "Liberty to all the world black and white." That footnoted the main fact, that the motivation of the maker was quite frankly stated to be "In order to perpetuate his memory in future ages." Silly as that sounds, and little as the fiddle had to recommend it otherwise, he wasn't entirely wrong, because here we are today talking about him, the better part of two centuries later. And his footnote is still very topical.

Since none of these makers, with the exception of the latter-day Guadagnini, had a really illustrious name, it seemed to me that the chances of these fiddles being spurious was slightly less certain than if their labels involved the names of Stradivari, Guarneri, Amati, or Stainer. I copied down the wording of the labels and decided to look them up, in my old violin books at home, before venturing to make any bid above a dollar for any of them.

One thing disturbed me. The bows with these violins were of the cheapest, shabbiest sort. One of them was stamped "Vuillaume," but its grip was that plain wrapping of brown leatheroid that you see on the bows included with beginners' outfits. Another was stamped "Tourte," and I remembered from my earliest readings in fiddle lore that the practice of marking their bows began in France only after the time of the Tourtes-père, Xavier, and François, and that John Dodd in England was the first of François Tourte's contemporaries to put his name on either frog or stick. Also, the cases were very beat-up, student-type, imitation-leather-covered boxes, and some of them were even stenciled, in whitewash-like paint, with the names and numbers of different school districts. Of course there was always the chance that genuine old fiddles had been put in cheap cases and paired with shoddy bows, just for auction purposes, but it was hardly likely. Besides, while I had never before been in that particular auction room, I had heard of it as the kind of place where they would "sign a Renoir while you wait."

When I checked my notes on the wording of the labels, they all squared with the facts about the various makers as given in my different fiddle books. The names were all spelled right, and the places and dates were the proper ones for those makers. Antonio Guadagnini was credited with being a not unworthy follower of his much more famous forebears, Lorenzo and the great "J. B.," and Marconcini was supposed to have been a friend of Paganini, though there was no record of any of his violins ever being used by Paganini in public. As for Felice Mori Costa, there was not much to go on about him, though I did find one of his fiddles pictured in the Jalovec volume, *Italian Violin Makers*.

I decided to hazard a hundred-dollar sealed bid on each, on the grounds that they could hardly be worth less, whatever they were, and on the off-chance of their being genuine, in which case my low bids would hardly serve as more than openers.

But then, as an afterthought, because of the more famous name,

I raised the bid on the Guadagnini to $135. I thought my hundred-dollar bid on that one might just possibly provoke a couple of five- or ten-dollar raises, simply on the fact that this was the one familiar name, and I thought I might as well allow for that. On the other hand, if it were genuine, and anybody who knew violins attended the auction, the odds were overwhelming that almost *any* Guadagnini would command at least ten times my bid.

As it turned out, the bidding was at least genuine, whether any of the fiddles were or not. I got four of the five violins, losing out only on the Irish one with the quaintly worded label. The Marconcini, the anonymous Stainer model, and the Guadagnini all came in at the prices I had bid for them, while I got the Mori Costa at ninety dollars, ten less than I had bid. This last was reassuring.

When I picked the fiddles up, on Monday morning after the auction, I brought them back to the office and stuck them up on the top shelves of my bookcase. Early mornings the rest of the week I tried them out, at a time when nobody but the night watchman could be disturbed by the din, and came to the conclusion that they were worth about what I had paid for them. I found the tone of the Marconcini harsh, and that of the nameless German specimen hollow, but the Mori Costa and the Guadagnini both had a good solid clear tone, though neither had the soft smooth mellowness of my Kloz.

But all these fiddles, though they were relatively low in value both intrinsically and from the viewpoint of the collector, had an interest for me that the Kloz had never had. With the sole exception of Stainer, who was closer to the Cremonese than any other Teutonic maker, the Tyrolese violin makers, and particularly those of Mittenwald, always seemed to me to be a pretty undistinguished lot, when considered purely as craftsmen. The enormous Kloz family made a great many sweet-voiced instruments, but with rare exceptions, chiefly afforded by Sebastian and occasionally Matthias, their fiddles aren't much to look at, and in general you can say that a Kloz looks like nothing so much as another Kloz. This is paradoxical, because the German makers generally were influenced mainly by the Stainer model. But whereas a genuine Stainer could readily be mistaken for an Italian instrument, the hundreds of Stainer copies made by German and Austrian makers in the eighteenth century all look heavily, grossly, and swollenly German. His own violins, exceedingly scarce now as indeed they have always been, are really no more highly arched, and no less gracefully, than those of the Brothers Amati, but the copiers of his model have never seemed able to avoid making it look tubby. And a Kloz, however sweet its tone, and mine was sweet, is still a Kloz.

Looking at it, as opposed to playing it, next to these four auction fiddles, none of which could equal it in tone, I could see in them the bloodlines, copies though they were, of the aristocracy of fiddledom. They all suggested, as the Kloz did not, the main lines that have been dominant in individual violin design over the past three centuries, the Stainer, the Amati, the Stradivari, and the Guarneri. And though they had cost me next to nothing, in terms of the current prices of genuine old violins, they had nevertheless served as sufficiently suggestive exemplars of these main model differences, to make me feel again in looking at them a reawakening response to the *lore* of the violin, just as playing the Kloz again and finding that I could still negotiate the four movements of the sixth Handel Sonata had reawakened me to its lure.

Lure and lore, by the time Rafael came to town for the February concert I was firmly hooked on both counts, and when he wanted to talk fishing I wanted to talk fiddles.

He had just then acquired, through his friend, William Moennig, from the estate of his late teacher at Curtis Institute, Lea Luboschutz, the magnificent specimen from that great year of the golden period, 1717, the Strad known as the Nightingale. Going around to the green room at Carnegie Hall before the concert to see it, to hold it, and even at his urging to play it—very tentatively and diffidently, the first two dozen notes of "my" Handel Sonata—gave me a sudden access of fiddle fever from which I may very well never recover.

THE FOUR AUCTION FIDDLES

Left to right: Amati model by Felix Mori Costa, Parma, 1809; Stainer model, unlabeled; Stradivari model, by Giuseppe Marconcini, Ferrara, 1822; and Guarneri model, by Antonio Guadagnini, Turin, 1851.

Henry Wolf

Rear view of the four auction fiddles, bought as copies (and probably copies of copies) of the four main models of violin design, Amati, Stainer, Stradivari, and Guarneri.

Henry Wolf

That was February 1966, and even though in the weeks and months immediately preceding I had begun reading up on the subject again, getting out my old fiddle books to look up labels, for instance, but then going on to read the books completely, I still think it was that close-up sight and touch and sound of the Nightingale that fused the magic moment, of making me the nympholept, of giving me the holy shudders, for the second time in my life.

That Rafael could truthfully observe that the Nightingale, in my hands, suffered a sudden transformation into the Crow did

THE NIGHTINGALE STRAD, 1717
Wm. Moennig & Son

nothing to abate my ardor. I had undoubtedly never before seen a Stradivari plain—I don't count the faraway glimpse of a gold-brown shape under the chin of a distant violinist on the concert stage—and the sight did something to me that I had never experienced before.

I recalled having read somebody's definition of a highbrow as being a man who has found something that interests him more than women, and while I had always gone far out of my way to avoid either being thought, or thinking of myself as, a highbrow, I could suddenly see some sense in the analogy.

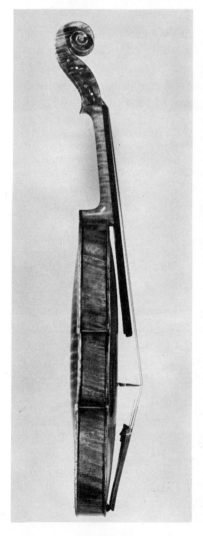 

George Szell, happening into the green room to ask Rafael something, turned to look at the "new" Stradivarius in its open case, to which I had returned it with the elaborate care of one returning a royal infant to its cradle, and said with a pale smile,

"Just what every good fiddler needs—a simple Strad."

Being some distance below the level of a good fiddler, even by the average man's standards, let alone those of a perfectionist like Szell, neither the sight of the fiddle itself nor the implications of that remark had stirred any acquisitive itch in me, and if you had told me then that I would have a Strad of my own before the year was out, I would have given you very high odds against it.

But I did, on looking at the other fiddle Rafael had, along with the Nightingale, in a double case (it was a copy of a Guarneri that had been made for him by William Moennig of Philadelphia, and was so inscribed inside), ask him if that was the same man who had issued a small publication that I had seen now and then called *The World of Strings*. And when Rafael said that it was, and that he had known Bill Moennig well since his student days at Curtis Institute and was in fact going to be seeing him in Philadelphia the next day, I asked him to see if Moennig could send me a few back copies of *The World of Strings*. Better still, remembering that I had cracked the head of my Albert Nürnberger bow trying to fiddle under one of the too-low ceilings of our house in the Village a few years before, I asked him to find out from Moennig what the chances might be of getting a bow with an ivory frog by John Dodd of Kew.

I suspected that a Dodd bow might cost more than all four of my auction fiddles, but had no idea how much more, not having kept up on the prices of fiddles or bows for many years. Rafael assured me that I would get a very square deal from Moennig on the bow whenever one might turn up, and there the matter was left.

I still felt a little diffident about spending any real money on a craze, which was the fairest word I could muster to characterize

RAFAEL DRUIAN WITH MOENNIG VIOLIN

Wm. Moennig & Son

this new fascination with fiddles. I remembered I had felt the same way for a long time about spending more than relatively small change on fishing, and how for years I had steadfastly refused to spend more than three or four dollars on a fly rod, confining my rare purchases in that category to the bargain stores on Forty-second Street, because I still felt some vague compunction, probably derived from my father's Mennonite heritage, about spending any real money on "foolishness."

God knows, if my relatively successful pursuit of fishing were to be classed as foolishness, then this would have to be classed as idiocy.

On the other hand, I had for years poured buckets of money into cars without qualms, or at least with far fewer than would have been warranted, because transportation costs can always be rationalized under the heading of necessity.

This tentative overture toward the acquisition of a new bow I now began to rationalize, on the conscious level, by recalling something I had read or heard about a pet saying of Ysaye's to the effect that any fool can manipulate the fingers of the left hand, but "the right hand is the artist."

Based on my proficiency with the left hand, it was undoubtedly true that the Kloz was still too good for me, but by the same token it was equally obvious that my right hand could use all the help it could get. QED. A new bow could now be regarded as a necessity.

But on the subconscious, or unacknowledged, level, the reason the new bow had to be a Dodd with an ivory frog, the choice of material for which can have no conceivable bearing on artistry or its lack, was that the one "find" I had ever made, as a kid who fancied himself a mighty violin hunter à la Tarisio, was a Dodd bow with an ivory frog. I had happened on it in a farmhouse some fifty years before, in the course of a Boy Scout hike, and it had been pronounced genuine by my friend Frank Stewart, the only known connoisseur of such things in the city of Grand Rapids, Michigan, and it had been bought and authenticated by Lyon & Healy of Chicago. (I now know, as I didn't then, that the man who certified it must have been Jay C. Freeman, who was Lyon & Healy's ranking expert then, around 1916, and until 1920, when he was lured away by Wurlitzer.)

Although I had been able to contemplate Rafael's Strad without wanting to possess it, or rather without even thinking about wanting to possess it, any more than I could be stirred by a particularly beautiful sunset into any thought or desire of possessing it, I recognized in myself the peculiar collector's itch that I felt stirring at the mere idea of having a Dodd bow with an ivory frog, like the one I had seen so long ago.

But if this were to become another seizure of the collecting fever, as I suspected it might before I ever heard a word from Moennig about it, then at least it wasn't a fiddle, but only a bow, and besides it was only a Dodd, and not a Tourte. I knew that at today's prices, collecting violins on the Strad or Guarneri level would be tantamount to collecting yachts, and I knew that even bows nowadays commanded prices that exceed those of all but a few of the violins that were pictured in the Lyon & Healy and Wurlitzer catalogs that were all I could afford to collect as a kid back in the teens and early nineteen twenties. I had in fact read of a Tourte bow for which Lee Wurlitzer, Rembert's widow, had refused all offers up to as high as $12,500.

So it was with a sense of relief that I heard from Moennig, a couple of months after the night of the Cleveland Orchestra concert when I had first seen Rafael's Strad, to say that on his European buying trip he had found me a Dodd bow with an ivory frog, and that the only hitch was that it would cost me $450. From the tone of his letter, and his saying "it seems there always has to be a hitch," I took it that he thought the price was high. But I had expected it to be more, because I thought I remembered that the one I had found in 1916 had been bought by Lyon & Healy for two hundred dollars, and judging by the way prices have gone up since then, I would have expected a comparable bow fifty years later to be at least a thousand. I thought I recalled that Tourtes at that time had run around four to five hundred dollars, and that, even a year or two after that, such top-dollar Strads as the famous Betts, which Mrs. Gertrude Clarke Whittal later gave to the Library of Congress, were going for from $12,500 to $15,000.

I hastened to assure Moennig that I wanted the Dodd bow, and that I would drive down to Philadelphia to pick it up, and would at the same time take advantage of my visit to show him my fiddles and get his expert opinion on the worth of my four auction "finds" and the Kloz.

Moennig's shop on Locust Street looks like a little eighteenth-century enclave in the middle of modern Philadelphia, as befits the age of the instruments he deals in, and I enjoyed the time I spent in the downstairs room waiting for him to come down from his office upstairs. There were counter and wall displays of fiddles and bows, and I sat down next to a vitrine in which there were a number of violin books I had never seen before. The girl at the switchboard offered to open it for me, when she saw me studying the titles, and I was soon lost in them.

There are, I have since learned, even more books on fiddles than there are on trout. But based on the total number of copies, I doubt that the lead would hold, because, though there are over three thousand titles, most violin books have been published either for subscribers, like Doring's extremely scarce *How Many Strads?*, or in rather severely limited editions, like the great book on Stradivari by the three Hill brothers, of W. E. Hill & Sons, of London. There is a paperbound reprint of that one, as it happens, and that's the only copy of it that I have, but the original big white volume, looking as if it might be a Debrett's Peerage or an Almanach de Gotha, that I found in Moennig's locked case, is now very hard to come by. There is a firm in London named Reeves that makes a specialty of reissuing some of these nearly legendary rare fiddle books of the past, but even their reprints, and those of the Amati Publishing Company, are themselves soon hard to find, unless you happen to get them as they come out. Even that isn't easy, because on a lot of these items, such as those advertised in *The Strad Magazine*, they have a nasty practice of restricting the orders to the United Kingdom only.

Moennig found me so engrossed in *La Casa Nuziale*, a book by Arnaldo Baruzzi about Stradivari's first house of his own, that he almost hesitated to interrupt my reading to show me the Dodd bow. But when I noticed him, an ebullient little man with glasses and a European style of haircut, I knew him on sight from his pictures in *The World of Strings*, and I couldn't wait to see the bow.

A Dodd bow is a thing of beauty, but my initial reaction was one of disappointment, because this ivory frog was much more finished than the more primitive one that I remembered. This one had mother-of-pearl eyes inset on each side, where the sides of the other, which I could still see in my mind after half a century, were completely plain. Also, this one had a mother-of-pearl slide and a metal ferrule enclosing the hair, and I was pretty sure that the one I remembered lacked both those features. In other words, this one looked much more like a modern bow.

Moennig readily conceded that there are many Dodd bows with plain-sided frogs, but doubted very much that the frog I de-

scribed fom memory could have been a violin bow. He said he'd
seen such frogs, lacking both the ferrule and the slide, with the
hair exposed along the under side to the point where it disap-
pears inside the frog, more often in double-bass bows, and very
occasionally in cello bows, but hardly ever in fiddlesticks, and he
couldn't remember seeing one by John Dodd, although he had
seen one or two by his father, Edward. He pointed out that this
frog was unlined (the metal lining being an innovation characteristic of the bows of François Lupot about 1800, and not
adopted by other makers, including Dodd and Tourte himself,
until later) and that it was stamped Dodd in four capital letters,
like the stamping on the stick. The stick itself, chocolate colored
and octagonal, with a beautiful hatchet head, was a full twenty-
nine and a half inches long, the length that has been standard
since the time of Tourte and that unfortunately the majority of
Dodd bows do not attain.

"A Dodd with an Ivory Frog"   *Henry Wolf*

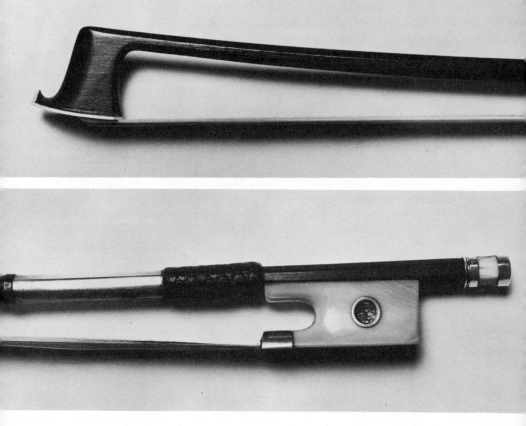

He offered to give my money back if I didn't want it. In my eagerness I had paid for it sight unseen, on first hearing from him that he had it. But of course I wanted it, and the more I looked at it the better I realized that this was in every way a much more finished piece of work than the only other Dodd bow I had ever seen. But, with a distinct sensation of the collector's itch, I heard myself saying that if he ever came across one with the plain-sided ivory frog I'd undoubtedly want that too.

When he began looking at my four auction fiddles, he wanted to know right away what I'd paid for them, and when I told him he laughed.

"Less than the price of the bow for all four—you couldn't go far wrong at that rate."

But he quickly dismissed them all as being, at least from the collector's point of view, virtually without value. They were all German, he said, with the possible exception of the yellow fiddle (the one labeled Antonio Guadagnini), and after taking that one over to the window for a closer look, he dismissed it too, as being not only not Italian but not even by a professional maker.

"Some amateur," he said, putting into the term all the contempt he could feel for those who were not, like himself, graduates of the Mittenwald school for violin makers.

What they might be worth to me to play on, assuming that I enjoyed playing any one of them, he felt was quite another matter, and he could see that all of them were capable of giving some satisfaction in this respect, quite apart from their lack of any interest as collector's items. Surrounded as he was by fiddles of real worth, he couldn't see any validity to my point about having these around as exemplars of the different schools of violin design. They were not that pure in model, he felt, though agreeing that among them they showed the main elements of the Stainer, Amati, Stradivari, and Guarneri influences. But they were not even exact enough, as copies, to have any real interest as mock-ups of those four seminal makes.

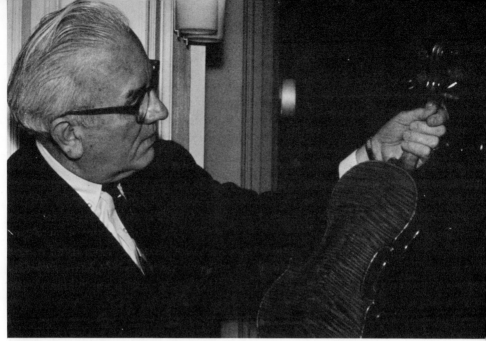

William Moennig of Philadelphia, in the Ashmolean Museum at Oxford, where the Messiah Stradivarius, most perfectly preserved of all Strads, is the keystone of the Hill & Sons Collection.

Wilda T. Moennig

The only real fiddle I had, according to him, was the Kloz. That was worth the other four put together, though not much more. When I pointed out that my wife had paid more than twice that much for the Kloz, buying it for me from a friend as long ago as 1936, he snorted,

"Hm, what a friend!"

He'd like to have a thousand dollars for every Kloz that had passed through his hands, but said he could count on the fingers of one hand those that ever touched or even came near that figure.

Still, he did pick up the Kloz again, and looked at it with greater interest. The back, particularly, seemed to command his attention for an inordinately long time.

"Have you ever thought that the back of this fiddle might be by somebody else?" he finally asked.

I hadn't. It was much handsomer than the belly, but that wasn't saying very much, because the top of my old Kloz was about as pretty as the proverbial mud fence. It was a dark and dirty brown, very grainy, and it didn't look as if it had ever been wiped off after use, as is customary with owners of cherished fiddles, by either me or any other of its presumed legion of owners back to 1734. But the back was that clear amber, a little darker than dairy-butter yellow, that I had always thought quite typical of Mittenwald violins. Its grain, from the join of its two pieces, flared slightly upward toward the sides.

"No," said Moennig, "if I had to bet on it I'd say that back wasn't made in Mittenwald, by Kloz or anybody else. I'd say it was made by Tieffenbrucker."

I thought he must be putting me on. It was a name I'd often read, but never heard pronounced, before. It is more often encountered in the alternate spelling Duiffoprugcar, and is always mentioned in all fiddle books in the chapter concerned with the origins of the violin. He was a Lyons luthier, active in the first years of the sixteenth century, well before either Andrea Amati or Gasparo da Salò was born, and hence for a long time given priority over them in the contention for the distinction of being the "inventor" of the violin. When it was finally determined that the only true violins attributed to him, as opposed to the marvelously inlaid viols for which he was famous, were fakes made presumably with puckish interest by J. B. Vuillaume, the greatest copyist who ever lived, the seriousness of his claim collapsed. But in the older fiddle books that I grew up on, he always enjoyed at least equal billing with the Brescian da Salò (or Bertolotti) and the Cremonese Amati, as one of the three most probable progenitors of the violin.

Moennig talks fast, and with some tendency to mumble and mutter, and when I pointed out that what he was saying could mean that the back was about two hundred years older than the rest of the Kloz, he said yes, he realized that would put it back "with Del Gesù and those other old fellows," but that he figured that Aegidius must have come upon an old back he liked,

and decided to build a fiddle around it. To bolster this contention, he pointed out that to fit the contour of the back, Kloz had
been forced into the making of some very un-Klozlike middle
bouts.

I thought about this all the way home. That Moennig is an expert surely nobody in the field will deny. He shares with Max
Möller of Amsterdam, Pierre Vidoudez of Geneva, and the late
Rembert Wurlitzer the craft credentials of being a violin maker
himself, and certainly he has seen and handled as many pedigreed
violins as anybody now active. Surely he *couldn't* have said, "Del
Gesù and those other old fellows." But my memory for words is
extremely tenacious, and I knew he said it. What he must have
meant, and must have thought he was saying, was, "Da Salò and
those other old fellows." That would have made sense, as Del
Gesù in that context did not.

Da Salò was active, right after Tieffenbrucker, in the last half of
the sixteenth century—he died in 1609—whereas Bill Moennig
certainly knows as well as he knows his own name that the great
Joseph Guarnerius del Gesù was not only still alive in 1734, the
date of my Aegidius Kloz, but had some of his greatest fiddles
still ahead of him, including the celebrated Cannon of Paganini,
which dates from 1743.

Stimulated by the new Dodd bow, which at least made me think
I was playing it better than I ever had before, I began giving the
Kloz more and more intensive workouts. And every time I
picked it up and laid it down I was intrigued by the new interest
Moennig had given its back.

If Moennig was right, or, rather, if there was any way of prov-
ing that Moennig was right, then my ugly duckling of a Kloz
would be transformed into a swan of world renown, for it would
constitute the missing link in the evolution of the violin from the
medieval viols.

Granted, a front would be a much more convincing missing link
to find than a back, for it is in the transformation of the crescent

sound holes of the viol into the uniquely characteristic f-holes of the violin that the essence of the metamorphosis lies. But certainly the Kloz was a normal violin in every other respect, and its compatibility with the Duiffoprugcar back would be strong presumptive evidence that once there must have been, somewhere, a true violin by Duiffoprugcar.

For the most part, I just fiddled with it—playing such snatches as I could remember of Austrian and Hungarian songs, from the cafés and czardas that I used to frequent so much when I was living over there for the first few years right after World War II. I always thought the Kloz would be a first-rate fiddle for a first-rate café fiddler—a *primas*, as they call them in Hungary. And remembering the best singers of those teary-beery, schmaltzy Viennese songs, such as Mahly Nagl, who was still singing in those days, I always think of the tone of the Kloz as a voice with a tear in it. It was the perfect fiddle, buttery-smooth and mellow, tinged with melancholy, for the kind of tunes I was playing on it. Digging among the lower layers of stuff I hadn't looked at in twenty years, I found some spiral-bound collections of then current favorites from Vienna and Budapest, and soon had between thirty and forty of them down pat, from memory, enough to keep me going by the hour. Since they didn't exceed the range of the soprano voice, the first three positions on the violin were adequate for their rendition, and since these were the lower limited range of the fiddle's reaches where I felt at all sure-fingered, they made just the right kind of music for both my fiddle and my long-ago-arrested degree of proficiency with it. I was, if not happy with my fiddling, because it never sounded the way I wanted it to sound, at least not beset by frustration at trying to contend with things that were over my head, violinistically speaking.

But every time I would vary my Austro-Hungarian repertory of easy tunes by trying to play again the things I had studied as a child, I would feel hampered by my limitations of technique. The only items of this type that I could recall *in toto*, apart from the Handel Sonata that had miraculously stayed with me all these years, were *Simple Aveu*, Thomé's *Simple Confession* that I had played for my mother's clubwomen, and Gabriel-Marie's *La*

40

Cinquantaine, the tinkly roundabout tune that Alec Templeton and I always used to play at his house in Greenwich. He used to give it such wonders of embellishment on the piano as to make the inept performance of my part on the fiddle sound almost good, and he always called it "our song."

Now I would play that, and the Handel Sonata in E Major, Number Six. But I didn't enjoy playing *Simple Confession*, even though I found that my fingers still knew their way through it. I would dismiss as headshrinking tomfoolishness any suggestion that the memory of my embarrasment on that early occasion still beclouded the tune itself, but I haven't felt like playing it again, after satisfying myself that I could.

In a recent conversation with Josef Szigeti I recalled a performance that he had given with the Cleveland Orchestra in 1956, and he surprised me by remembering it.

"Not at all surprising," he said, "I remember that occasion so distinctly because I was unhappy with that concert—you always remember best the things that make you unhappy at the time."

I suppose this is just another facet of the thought that good generals learn more from their defeats than from their victories, but I'm not sure, because I thought the Szigeti performance with Szell was superb, and maybe what made him unhappy that night was something else entirely.

In any case, my own unhappiness with the violin did not sufficiently outweigh the pleasure I got from fiddling with the Kloz—particularly as enhanced by the addition of the Dodd bow—to make me decide to do anything about it.

True, every time I played the sixth Handel Sonata I found myself wishing that I knew the other five, and every time I heard any Mozart, on the car radio or on a phonograph, I wished that I knew some on the violin, but I thought that not having studied these things in my youth they were no longer within my reach, and I would remind myself that one definition of happiness is being content with what you've got.

TWO

Within the month after I had been down to Moennig's to get the Dodd bow, Rafael called me from there, to remind me of our conversation the night I had first seen his Strad. He had found a fiddle for me that they had just got in, and he had been trying to persuade Moennig to send it up to me to try, but "Bill was being diffident about it," and didn't want to do it unless I would first express some interest in seeing it.

I remembered now that Rafael had been touting Guadagninis that night as the coming instruments, and particularly the J. B. as the coming concert violin. His point was that the later Strads and Guarneris, in addition to being priced out of the reach of all but the fattest cats among both collectors and performers, were also presumably nearing the peak of their effectiveness in terms of their probable life-span as concert instruments. Since they all belong to the first half of the eighteenth century, and the best J. B. Guadagninis cluster around the midpoint of the century's latter half, then the Guads are a better investment from the player's viewpoint, as they may safely be assumed to have left in them at least one more playing generation than have the Strads and Del Gesù.

I thought this was dubious reasoning, remembering that I had been reading for years, in books dating back the better part of a hundred years, that the "probable" life span of the great Cremonese violins, not as objects of art but as effective playing instruments, would be from two and a half to three centuries. But nobody knows this, and nobody could prove it, and certainly there are a lot of very old fiddles that seem to disprove it. The bulk of the Da Salòs and Magginis, and the Andrea Amatis, and for that matter the Brothers Amati, date from before 1600, and certainly they show no signs of being played out. On the contrary, it could be argued that they have gone on acquiring greater mellowness and sweetness of tone. Recently I played a Gasparo da Salò that must be four hundred years old, and a more vigorous violin would be hard to find. I say "must be" because the Brescian violins were not dated, either in Da Salò's time or in that of his younger contemporary, Gio. Paolo Maggini, whereas the Cremonese always were dated, from Andrea Amati's day onward; but, because Da Salò died in 1609, any violin of his must be at least three hundred and sixty years old, or a good century beyond that "probably maximum optimum" age that has been predicted with such remarkable unanimity by so many fiddle writers for so long a time.

That night with Rafael, when he seemingly invoked this old argument as a reason in support of the current tendency to tout the J. B.'s, I said I could almost wish it were true, because then maybe the price of an Amati would come back down within reason.

Since I play in a room and not a hall, I would never have any need for one of the big-voiced violins, like the Strads after 1700, or the later Del Gesù, or Bergonzis, or the J. B.'s of the Turin period. What I would like, I said that night, would be one of those wonderful old yellow violins of the seventeenth century, soft-voiced and mellow—the kind that had been played in chambers or in the cells of monks, rather than in courts or concert halls. Such a fiddle, I fancied, would give my playing another such lift as the purely momentary and perhaps illusory one that I thought I had felt the few moments I played Rafael's Strad.

And just such a fiddle, according to Rafael, Moennig now had, and not at a king's ransom either. It wasn't an Amati, but it "only just barely wasn't an Amati," according to Rafael—because it was a Cappa.

Rafael tends to joke a lot, even when he isn't joking. But I got the point of that one. A genuine Giofreda Cappa is rarer than an Amati today, for the simple reason that the bulk of his output has been "passing" as Amatis for the last three hundred years. The fame of the Amatis had permeated all the courts of Europe while Stradivari was still in swaddling clothes, and law actions over the palming-off of a fraudulent fiddle as a genuine Amati go back before 1700.

So how much was this almost-Amati, I wondered, and Rafael

MISS WARREN'S GIOFREDA CAPPA
Wm. Moennig & Son

said it was only four thousand dollars, with a Hill certificate thrown in. And the color, he added, remembering my other desideratum, was "like light toast, thickly buttered."

I had heard enough, and the fiddle came within the week, by REA Protective Signature Service, a sort of courier delivery to which valuable instruments are quite commonly consigned.

The Hill certificate, showing that the violin had been sold to "Miss Warren of Deal," not otherwise identified, in 1888, testified to the belief of W. E. Hill & Sons that the instrument was a characteristic production of Giofreda Cappa in Saluzzo "about 1680," although the label plainly read "1683," and added that "we do not fancy the scroll to be original."

I could imagine Miss Warren, tall and stately as Tennyson's Maud, and from the tone of the fiddle I could imagine her playing, as they used to say of Maud Powell, "like an angry man." There was nothing feminine about the Cappa, other than the

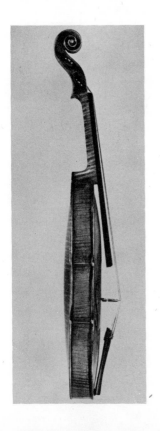

recorded fact that it had once belonged to a woman. I found its tone silvery and hard, if not actually harsh, and in no way suggestive of the limpid, almost liquid-smooth softness that I had always dreamed of getting from an Amati.

I kept it with the understanding that if Moennig ever found me anything more truly Amati-like, or more nearly what I had come to expect of an Amati, I could turn the Cappa back in on it for full price.

The Kloz was now relegated to the office, with three of the four auction fiddles, and the Cappa was brought home, to try to compete for a place in Janie's affections with the little red fiddle, the ninety-dollar Mori Costa, the only one of all my fiddles to date that she liked.

Since the Mori Costa was the cheapest of the lot, and followed fairly faithfully the main features of the Grand Pattern Amati, perhaps it was by projection from that that I had built the dream-tone of an Amati in my mind. But whatever it was, certainly the Cappa, at forty-four times the price, was not it.

The first time I played it at home, Janie yowled. In fairness, I should explain that seemingly ungallant term by saying that her hearing *is* doglike. She is cursed with perfect pitch and super-human hearing. Those little dog whistles, that are supposed to be so far above the range of human hearing—well, she hears them before the dogs do: Hey, wake up, Fido, the whistle's blowing. A more unfortunate mate for a man of my fiddling pertinacity could hardly be conjured up for horror-story purposes.

When Rafael heard of this contretemps, he came to the lady's rescue with the gift of a practice mute so heavy that it effectively decapitated the Cappa's tone, and restored to the household a sort of uneasy peace—the term being used only in its relative sense, as indicating the absence of actual war—that endured for the matter of months that the Cappa was accorded house room.

I read up on Cappa at every opportunity but found the references endlessly confusing. According to some of the books, Giofreda Cappa, with the first name spelled four or five different ways, died in 1640; according to others, he was born in 1644, the same year as Stradivari, and died at 73 in 1717, twenty years earlier than Stradivari. According to some authors, there were two Cappas, father and son, of the same name, but according to others, this one's father's name was Andrea. (A sort of Gresham's law seems to prevail in violin literature, with every author's mistakes copied a dozen times more frequently than his accurate statements, with the result that the Cappas probably never will be straightened out, any more than the Guadagninis are now. The recent Jalovec two-volume *Encyclopedia of Violin Makers* still lists two J. B. Guadagninis, although this was cleared up decades ago by Ernest Doring's *The Guadagnini Family of Violin Makers*.)

Cappa is presumed to have been a pupil of Nicolo Amati, as Stradivari himself must still be presumed to have been. But in Stradivari's case there are at least a couple of labels, in violins of 1665 and 1666, that bear the phrase "alumnus Nicolaij Amati," whereas no such evidence has survived to say the same for Giofreda Cappa. Of course, so few of his labels have survived, most having been succeeded by false Amati labels, that there is always the possibility that even more of his earliest labels may have borne his master's name, but it is extremely unlikely that any would ever show up at this late date. In any case, his violins remained so much more constant to the Amati model than even the earliest Strads, the so-called *amatisé* fiddles of the 1665–1690 period, that the marvel is that his work survives in its own right at all.

I felt the same sense of wonder in reaction to the statement in the Hill certificate that the Cappa's scroll was not original. When you realize that every old violin, in playing condition, that was made before the last years of the eighteenth century, has had its neck lengthened, its fingerboard extended, and its bass bar replaced by a longer and stronger one, to meet the increased pressure on the belly of modern pitch and the widened range of music, it is remarkable, not that so many didn't get their original heads put back on, but that so many did.

As shown in David Boyden's *The History of Violin Playing* (and as demonstrated in a record inserted in the volume's slip-case), Hill's have kept a Stainer, purely for exhibition purposes, in its original playing condition, with the shorter neck, raised short fingerboard and small bass bar that were standard on all violins made before 1765. It is the exception that proves the rule, and it is fascinating to hear it, as played by Alan Loveday on the demonstration record, with its lower pitch and softer tone, in contrast to a Strad that has had the customary modernization.

Hearing it, I thought that must have been what I really had in mind, when I kept longing for what I thought of as the true Amati sound all the months I was struggling with the Cappa.

THREE

As I had told Mr. Moennig on the day I was down in Philadelphia picking up the Dodd bow, getting that bow was a dream come true; but what I really knew would always be lurking in the back of my mind was a dream fiddle, and I described it to him, just as something he could be keeping his eye out for, whether it took him a matter of months or of years to find.

It should be an old Italian violin with a sweet small voice, and I imagined it would probably date from some time before 1650, which would mean stopping short of the Grand Pattern Amatis both in date and in price, as I hoped to limit my expenditure for it to somewhere between four and five thousand dollars. Pointing to the back of my Kloz, I said that would serve as a sample for the mellow old yellow I saw in my mind's eye, but that this detail was less important than the softness and sweetness of its tone. Probably it would be a lady's fiddle, or maybe a nun's, at any rate something of which it would never be expected that its voice would fill more than a drawing room or perhaps the chapel of a convent. Hopefully I thought of something Italian, of the vintage of the Brothers Amati, which would bring it to a date more nearly of the time when the Pilgrims landed on Plymouth Rock, and in any case before 1630, when Hieronymus Amati died. I was pretty sure I didn't want anything as piercing as a Stainer, or as full bodied as a Nicolo Amati after 1640, even if considerations of cost didn't rule both those possibilities out. (I had heard even then of Grand Pattern Amatis bringing twenty thousand dollars, and have since heard of one going for twenty-five thousand.)

I was going about this very much the way people do when they first start talking with their architect about how little they want to spend on remodeling that little old farmhouse—after all, it's hardly more than a shack, and they wouldn't want to tie up a small fortune in it, though of course they ought to realize that this is exactly what they'll wind up doing anyway, no matter what anybody says beforehand.

But as long as I confined my collecting to bows, I figured that I would at least decimate the damages, as fiddles generally cost at least ten times as much.

The Cappa had met all my dream fiddle's specifications except age, on which it had missed the mark by some thirty years, but I soon knew that it wasn't the answer, as I found that I went right on dreaming while playing it, like one who goes on fantasizing even while engaged in active intercourse.

I kept telling myself that I was liking it better and better the more I played it, but this was a hard form of autotherapy to sustain, as Janie's hoots and catcalls and Bronx cheers were not perceptively dwindling, even after the compassionate installation of the heavy practice mute on the instrument's bridge.

"You sound dreadful," she said, adding ruminatively, "even when you play fairly well."

The poor Cappa. I began feeling even sorrier for it than for myself. It had undoubtedly led a more placid life in the presumably less rambunctious ambiance of the eighteen eighties, when it was in the genteel embrace of Miss Warren of Deal.

But the Dodd bow with the ivory frog was an unalloyed delight, giving my right hand an unaccustomed, and, according to Janie, unwarranted, sense of prowess. She said its effect on my fiddling was not noticeable, while I felt I was wafting it like a veritable fairy wand, and inside my head the sound was celestial, at least in those rare moments when my left hand did nothing untoward to mar it.

Within a couple of months, however, even that light of my life began to dim, as the screw nut ceased to function. It would turn, but beyond midpoint the tension would not lessen.

One of my teachers had so impressed upon me, over fifty years before, the extreme importance of never putting a bow away without first relaxing all tension on it, completely, that through the years I had never once failed to do so. And now, ironically, the first time I had a really good bow in my stewardship, I was for the first time not obeying that stern admonition. Being of a conformist nature, I had always treated cheap German and Japanese bows as if they were Tourtes, and now, after my nightly turn with the Dodd, I had to lay it away untended in this respect.

As it happened, the bow had been at about mid-tension when the screw nut stopped functioning, so my actual use of it was unaffected, and obviously the actual strain on the stick was nowhere nearly as great as if it had been screwed up tight, the way Kreisler used to keep his, at a point where the curve approached convexity.

So I wrote Moennig asking if it was all right to leave it that way, or if I should send it back for him to do something about it.

Ever the gentleman, Moennig replied that of course the bow needed attention, but that he hated to deprive me even for a week of such extreme pleasure as I was obviously deriving from its use, so he was sending me to use, while mine was back for repair, the other of the two John Dodd bows he had acquired in the collection from which mine came.

This one had a tortoiseshell frog and gold mountings, where mine had ivory and silver. It had a round stick, instead of the octagon shaping that mine had, and was a half-centimeter shorter.

I knew that the ivory frogs were much more common, over the whole run of Dodd's production, than the tortoiseshell ones, and I understood that of these latter, with gold mountings, he had made only a few for specially favored clients, but I nevertheless hoped that its slightly shorter length and the round stick would tend to offset these advantages to some extent, and that I could have this bow for not too much more than I had paid for mine.

I knew that I didn't have to buy it, since he had simply sent it to me to use while mine was being fixed, but it never occurred to me that something he had himself so recently acquired (it had been under three months since the European buying trip on which he had obtained both of them) should not be for sale at all. But that turned out to be the case. Moennig not only would not name a figure, he simply wouldn't consider selling the gold-mounted, tortoiseshell-frogged Dodd at any price. Yet it was his own idea, and not mine, to lend it to me to use for nothing.

It gave me a new insight into the psychology of violin dealers. I had assumed, too blithely, as it turned out, that anything a dealer offered to let me use would also, automatically, be offered for sale. But remembering reading about the Tourte that Lee Wurlitzer would not part with at any price, I realized that in the fiddle trade there must be some values that these people cherish more than money. Moennig simply said that for years he had been trying to amass a collection of prime examples of bows of the different makers, to be used in future for purposes of identification, and that he had been determined from the moment of their acquisition to keep one or the other of these two Dodds. He made me feel a little better about it by saying that if I had not made such a Freudian thing out of insisting that my Dodd had to have an ivory frog, that would have been his own choice as the one to be held back from sale, and he would have offered me the other; but since I was not offering to trade that one back in for this tortoiseshell one, he would have to keep it. He had me there. I'd have been about as ready to give up my right arm. He hoped I wouldn't be angry, but there it was.

Angry, no; disappointed, yes. The only thing at that moment that I wanted more than one Dodd bow was two Dodd bows, and since the gold wrapping and mounting of the second one were so compatible with the gold peg insets and gold tailpiece shield of the Cappa, I had counted on using that one at home (with perhaps still some doggedly lingering hope of thereby lowering the decibels of the din upsetting my captive audience) and the ivory-frogged one at the office with the Kloz.

Typical of the way the man in the clutch of any collecting mania rationalizes his whims, I now said I'd settle for a gold-mounted Tubbs bow, whether or not made for W. E. Hill & Sons, and whether with tortoiseshell, ivory, or ebony frog. What had started by accident was now pursued by design. If the steel shaft that fits inside the cap had not come loose on my Dodd, on which I was fiddling so happily every night at home, it would never have occurred to me that I "needed" another bow for the office. But getting in as I do at six-thirty, where none of the gentry ever show up before nine-thirty, and my secretary seldom before ten, obviously I have more actual fiddling time there most mornings than I have most nights at home. So the matter of another bow suddenly became urgent.

Moennig was quick to oblige, with a prewar Hill bow, one of their famous fleur-de-lis, gold-mounted, with tortoiseshell frog, and I was quick to take it. But I was just as quick to give it back, because within the month Moennig came up with *two* John Dodds.

He explained that they really should be sold as a pair, because that was how they had been held for many years. One was what I had been hollering for, gold-trimmed with an ivory frog, and the other, silver-trimmed with an ebony frog. What made them a pair was that they both had ebony-bordered ivory headplates. Best of all was the price of the pair, which was only seven hundred and fifty dollars, making one of them virtually "free," as I could turn the Hill back in for the three hundred and seventy-five I had paid for it.

Far be it from me to be the one to break the pair, I thought, and besides, I could think of one of them as already paid for. So, by invoking the rationale peculiar to all collectors, I could really tell myself that I was getting one of them "for nothing" and only paying for the other, making one of them a sort of extra dividend.

I wrote Moennig right back with the news that went without saying, that I wanted them both, amending my former remark on this subject (on the occasion of losing out on the Dodd with the tortoiseshell frog) by saying that, as of now, if I could think of anything I wanted more than a Dodd bow it could only be two Dodd bows, and adding the gratuitous information that his letter had made an otherwise foggy and grey-blue October Monday turn suddenly merry and bright. In my exuberance I called him Sweet William.

He answered by return mail, sending on the certificates giving the detailed descriptions of each of the two "new" Dodds, and saying that the bows were following under the same REA Protective Signature Service that had brought me the Cappa.

Surely, anticipation is one of the chief delights of any form of collecting, and by way of savoring the waiting period between the receipt of the certificates and the arrival of the bows themselves I began reading up on John Dodd of Kew all over again.

Despite the startling rise in bow prices, which have gone up in recent years even more sharply than the prices of violins, there are still very few books about them. Compared to the three thousand books on the violin, there are only three, at least in English, on the bow. The newest, *Bows and Bow Makers*, by

William C. Retford, was published in 1964 by The Strad, London, under the imprint of W. E. Hill & Sons, for whom Retford, then ninety years old, had made bows for many years. The classic, called simply *The Bow*, by Henry St. George, was also published by The Strad, but many years ago, and is long out of print, and I don't yet have the long-promised reprint from Reeves of London, who have been slow in following their announced schedule of reprints. But I did have a copy in my office of the third one, *Bows for Musical Instruments of the Violin Family*, by Joseph Roda, published in 1959 by Wm. Lewis & Son, Chicago. In looking at the Dodd spread on plate 6 in that volume I suddenly realized, in reading the descriptive captions beneath the bows pictured as numbers 29 and 30, that I was looking at my own new matched pair, before they had even reached me from Philadelphia.

There they were, large as life, number 29 with "a round stick, ivory frog with gold mountings," and number 30, "octagonal stick, ebony silver mounted. Branded on frog and stick." Both frogs had plain sides, without the more usual mother-of-pearl eye, and the joy of recognition was overwhelming. I felt like an immigrant at the dock, catching sight of a relative he hasn't seen for fifty years, for I saw that in the gold-mounted one with the ivory frog I would have a very near mate to the Dodd bow I had "discovered" when I held it in my hands in a West Michigan farmhouse near Berlin (later changed to Marne, after we got into the war with Germany the next year) during a pause in a Boy Scout hike. And at that moment, no matter what it cost, I would have felt recompensed for waiting, without consciously realizing I was waiting, for it was fifty years almost to the day, from the fall of '16 to the fall of '66.

I was sure that after a thrill like that, the arrival of the bows themselves could only be anticlimactic, following as it did by several days the orgy of appreciation of them in which I had indulged.

Both sticks were only fractionally shorter than my first Dodd bow, which was exceptional in that so many of the Dodd violin

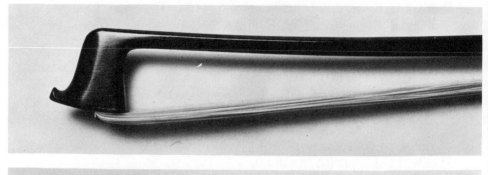

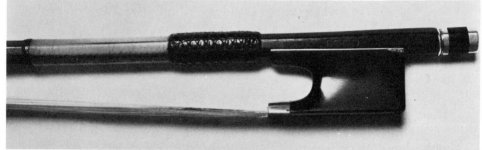

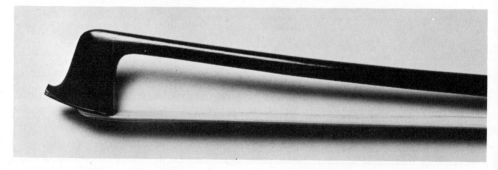

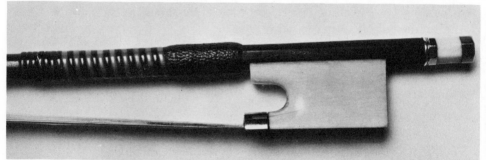

THE MATCHED PAIR OF DODDS   *Henry Wolf*

bows do fall appreciably short of the standard length as established by the peerless Tourte at 73 centimeters, or 29½ inches.
My first one, at 72.8 centimeters very nearly met this norm,
and of these two, the ivory with gold trim came to 72.5 centimeters and the silver-mounted ebony, to 72. Despite this, and
the memory-associations with the plain-sided ivory frog, I found
the shorter of these two even more congenial as a playing stick,
though I like them both.

Dodd, long known as "the English Tourte," was the first contemporary in England of the great Tourte himself to become
famous on the Continent, and for a long time was the only one.
I remembered a phrase quoted by Antoine Vidal in *La Lutherie
et les Luthiers* about Dodd, and credited to a doctor in Richmond who knew him, that "he was most regular in his irregular
habits" and citing his fondness for a mixture of gin and beer
called "purl." He died in his eighty-eighth year in 1839 at the
Richmond workhouse, although he was actually buried not there
but in Kew, and when they asked him on his deathbed which he
was, Catholic or Protestant, he said, as he might have said of the
choice of gin and beer, "a little of both."

Retford, as a bowmaker himself, dismisses all the Dodds, including the great John of Kew, as makers of bows that must now be
regarded as obsolete, and of interest only to collectors, almost
like the bows of Corelli's day. But perhaps because I am better
endowed as collector than player, I can't credit this at all. And
Rafael Druian, who is certainly more competent to speak for
players than I could ever be for collectors, has so long and
loudly envied me my first Dodd, though he has two Tourtes
(father and son), a Lupot, and a Sartory, that I finally had to
will it to him, to stop his pressing me to sell it to him, from the
moment he found out that I had two others.

I took all three of the Dodds, along with the Cappa, out to Cleveland at Thanksgiving time, where Jane and I normally spend the
holiday weekend at the house of her cousin, Kay Williams, and
there in a high upstairs room well out of earshot of everybody,
Rafael and I fiddled by the hour, as he rashly undertook to cor-

rect, in a couple of days, the bad habits that had become endemic to my playing over the course of decades.

For one thing, I clutched the fiddle's neck with a grip like that of a drowning man, with the result that I had developed a callus between my thumb and forefinger, at that edge of the palm where the lifeline begins, almost the size of a thimble. Rafael tried to break me of the habit of strangling the fiddle with this death grip by thinking of its neck as something not to be squeezed, but to be hung from, like a strap in the subway. He tried to make me feel as if my whole weight were hanging from the fingers themselves, and not from my grasp. Bringing the elbow around in under the violin, and not out at an angle to it as I had always held it, forced the fingers up over, above the fingerboard, instead of clutching away from it, as my panic grip had forced them to be.

I found this mental trick, of making myself feel that I was hanging from the fiddle's neck with my fingers alone, rather than grabbing at it between my thumb and forefinger and squeezing, did more to help get me out of the mud in which my fingering had been mired for fifty years than everything ever done by a succession of despairing teachers in my youth, in all their vain efforts to move me along out of the class where I was stuck, as a sort of permanent beginner.

Little else stayed with me, of other tricks he tried to give me, to serve as shortcuts to added proficiency, but perhaps that is not surprising, in view of the proverbial difficulty of imparting new tricks to an old dog.

He tried, for instance, to get me to dispense with that unnecessary crutch, the shoulder pad. I had always marveled at the sight of good fiddlers holding the violin in an upward tilted position, with nothing but air space between it and their shoulders. In fact, I had long ago come to spot this, as the most immediately distinguishable difference between the pro and the amateur, before either of them draws a bow across the strings. But knowing it, and being able to do it, are vastly different things, and I still

RAFAEL DRUIAN WITH
THE NIGHTINGALE
Now Associate Dean of
the Music School at the
California Institute of
the Arts, Los Angeles,
this picture was taken
shortly after his ac-
quisition of the famous
Nightingale Strad,
when he was Concert-
master of the Cleve-
land Orchestra.
Hastings-Willinger

use a Resonans Number Three shoulder pad, the highest of the three sizes they come in. Whenever I try to dispense with it, I get a frantic Chicken-Little conviction that the fiddle is about to fall, and nothing I can tell myself can make me feel otherwise. Yet I remember, from dozens of times I saw him play, how Kreisler used to hold his, higher than anybody, at about the angle of a Bofors antiaircraft gun, without any visible means of support other than resting it on his lapel, about where one would have judged his collarbone to be, and it stayed there as if planted.

But the new sense of freedom and ease of motion for my fingers that I began to enjoy immediately after adopting the "hanging from the fiddle" attitude, and thereby relaxing the former death grip, enabled me to negotiate passages at a gallop that I had never been able to lope through before at a trot, and within a matter of weeks that old callous tissue began to be transferred, from the edge of my palm, where it didn't belong, to the pads of my fingers, where it did.

At the same time, and indeed for the first time, I found myself doing what all my teachers had tried in vain ever to get me to do, that is, to play "in the strings," so to speak, as opposed to just playing lightly on them.

The fact that my fingers were now curved up high over the fingerboard, rather than creeping up on it from the side, gave them a natural added leverage, and it now was both easier and also seemed to be more instinctive to press them down harder on the strings. It also made it seem much easier and more natural to use a vibrato, even on the short notes, than it ever had been before. I had always tended to forget, in my anxiety over getting each finger down in the right place, to vibrate and thus impart that succession of minute alterations of the pitch that builds up the richness of the tone.

I sensed that Rafael was discouraged that he had been able to teach me so little after such intensity of effort, but I on the other hand was amazed that he had been able to alter so much of what was wrong with my basic approach to the production of tone from a violin.

In the ensuing weeks, as the calluses were redistributed on my left hand, I found that I didn't have to press half as hard with my right hand, to get a reasonably intense tone, now that I was pressing that much harder with the fingers of my left.

FOUR

Wallowing in good bows now, I still had no better fiddle than the Cappa, but, thanks to Rafael's help, that was beginning to sound better, at least, than I had been able to make it sound before.

I felt, too, that much of the improvement in the sound must be due to the use of better bows than I had ever had, and hoped that soon a Brothers Amati violin might be turned up by Moennig that would do as much for my left hand as the Dodd bows seemed to me to have done for my right.

Joseph Wechsberg had been in town a few weeks before, on his annual visit from Vienna, where he has now lived for a number of years. I knew that he had at one time had an Antonius and Hieronymus Amati of the year 1608, and I asked him where it might be now. He said that he had sold it back to Emil Herrmann, who would undoubtedly know its present where-abouts.

I had duly passed this tip on to Moennig, who said that Herrmann was in Europe and far from well, and that he doubted much could be done in that direction, but that he was still looking and hoped to have some news for me soon.

When I got back from the Thanksgiving holiday in Cleveland at the beginning of December, a letter from Moennig was waiting for me, and it was indeed full of news. His letters are cheery and discursive, interlarded with puns and Pennsylvania folksayings, and studded with homespun analogies like "man who has a suit for every day of the week—and he has it on."

This one began with the surmise that there might still be a Santa Claus. No, he wasn't about to tell me that he had found a fiddle by the Brothers Amati, but something even more wonderful:

There had again come into his possession a very lovely *Antonio Stradivari*, and would I please not say I couldn't afford it until I had read his letter through to the end. He then proceeded to recount its history, as he himself had first had it in 1951 from Max Möller of Amsterdam.

The violin was made in 1672, when Stradivari was only 28, and still very much under the Amati influence. About 1890, when it was in the possession of George Hart, this well-known English dealer sold it to his personal friend George Gudgeon, a collector who was an excellent judge of fine instruments. A few years later Lady Tennant, of Grosvenor Square, London, who already had a Strad of the year 1699, pursuaded Mr. Gudgeon to sell her this one. She kept it until 1925, when Max Möller, Sr., bought it as well as her 1699 Stradivari, which is still known as the Lady Tennant Strad. It was next sold to Erna Rubinstein, the concert artist, who played it all over Europe for a decade.

Mr. Möller added that it was one of the five Strads that either he or his father had ever seen which had neither a sound-post patch nor any half-edging. These are items on the underside of a violin's table, or top, that nearly all old fiddles have needed to have installed because of the frequency of removal of the top for sound-post and bass-bar replacement or adjustment and other reconditioning.

Moennig went on to say that this violin had the sweet responsive tone that he knew I was seeking, and that he thought the price was equally sweet, because it was only twelve thousand five hundred dollars, an exceptionally low figure for a Strad, now that Grand Pattern Amatis were pretty generally hovering around the twenty-thousand mark. He pointed out that taking the Cappa back in trade for the four thousand I had paid for it would bring the actual cash outlay needed for this Strad down to the really reasonable figure of eighty-five hundred dollars. And he added that he would like to send it to me for trial.

My God. As high as I had dared to dream was a Brothers Amati, and here was a Strad *amatisé*. A Lady Tennant Strad—a famous name I'd known for years. I pinched and poked at Moennig's letter, as if to dispel a very real doubt that it was more than an optical illusion. Obviously, it could permit of but one answer, which was to send the blessed thing on for a trial that I knew would be only a formality.

How I would pay for it was another matter entirely, but there was a bank downstairs in our building that I had never really cased with an eye to robbery. That was one of the gambits I was ready to consider, in the state of dithering frenzy that Moennig's letter induced.

After I had written my answer, and it had been signed and sent, I realized that it had confused its terms, because I had referred to the fiddle both as *amatisé* and as the Lady Tennant Strad. The first was all right, because all Strads before 1684, the year of Nicolo Amati's death, are termed *amatisé* and the appellation is even extended almost to 1690, or until succeeded by *allongé*, for the Long Pattern with which he experimented for the better part of the next decade, until the Grand Pattern of the golden period was fully formed by about 1700. But the second, the Lady Tennant, was not all right, as that term is preempted, of course, by her 1699 Strad, which is well into the beginning of the golden period and not *amatisé* at all.

But the more I reflected on this, the more I felt a sensation of *déjà vu*, because it occurred to me that somewhere, and some time before, had I not already read about this second fiddle of Lady Tennant's?

I began looking through all the books I could think of in which I might possibly have read about this earlier Strad, such as the books on Stradivari by Henley and the brothers Hill, and the Hill edition of Baruzzi's *La Casa Nuziale*, about the house where he lived and worked from 1667–1680, but nowhere could I find any mention of this 1672 violin. Yet, as I kept looking, the surer I became in my own mind that I had read about this Lady Tennant fiddle somewhere. I even thought I remembered having read somewhere before about its having belonged to Erna Rubinstein, and the connection with Max Möller was also familiar.

I went back to Moennig's letter about it again and again, looking for some further clue to guide me for further search, and finally found it in the word "again." It had escaped me at the very beginning, where he told me that there had "again" come into his possession a very lovely Antonio Stradivari. That was the key to my dilemma, and it sent me back to Moennig's own little publication, *The World of Strings*, where I found the whole story, even with a picture of the violin in question, in a 1962 issue.

They still printed the prices of the instruments pictured in *The World of Strings* in those days, before all prices began to go up as fast as they have in recent years. Now prices are given on request, but no longer printed along with the description and picture.

But there it was, right below the whole *histoire*—$15,000, for the same violin that he was now offering me, four years later, for twenty-five hundred less. The entry read, in its entirety, beside the three pictures—front, side, and rear views—and the caption, "Antonio Stradivari, Cremona 1672," as follows:

> ex-"Lady Tennant," ex-"Erna Rubinstein." From the highly regarded Amsterdam firm of Max Möller we learn this Stradivari was acquired for Lady Tennant from the famous English collector, George Gudgeon. He, in turn, had pur-

chased it from the London dealer of high repute, George Hart, about 1890. In the year 1925 it appeared in the hands of the Russian violinist, Erna Rubinstein, who toured all of Europe. In a letter to us from Max Möller his closing remark is "hope and trust it will serve well one of the many talented violinists of your country." We expect to fulfiill that wish.

Maybe Moennig had fulfilled it, when he sold the fiddle that time, but he certainly wasn't going to come within shouting distance of it this time. Perhaps with exquisite tact, or perhaps simply to avoid giving me a too-convenient out against his offer of a trial, he had omitted that closing remark of Max Möller's, in quoting him in the letter to me. For one reason or another he had obviously thought it best not to raise any question concerning the niceties of worthiness to own such a noble instrument.

The sight of the violin itself, even in the small black-and-white pictures of *The World of Strings*, served to whet my anticipation of the sight of the actual fiddle, and I began working on a rationale as to why it might be all right for me to have it.

As a player, I felt that I was still not worthy even of the Kloz. But it did help a little, I felt, that this was only Lady Tennant's second violin.

So I beguiled my time until at last it came, under the REA Protective Signature Service, on December 12.

At first sight I was speechless. I had not been prepared, even after seeing the pictures of it in *The World of Strings*, for the fact that the sound holes would be so purely Stradivari, and in no way even suggestive of those of his master Amati. In 1672, Nicolo Amati still had another dozen years to live, and many of the later Amatis are presumed to be in large part the work of Stradivari. But in his own work, it was evident in these graceful apertures, which are to the personality of the violin at least as much as the eyes are to the face, Stradivari was already very much his own man.

THE GUDGEON STRAD, 1672
Wm. Moennig & Son

The belly, as so often is the case with old violins, was slightly
darker than the sides and back, which were the transparency of
amber compared to its rich golden brown. The maple of the
sides and scroll was quite plain, typical of his earliest instruments,
before he had acquired the gorgeously flamed wood that so en-
hances the later specimens, but the back was nicely flamed, of

two pieces, with rather small curls ascending very slightly up-ward from the center joint.

The scroll, of extreme delicacy, was the most Amati-like thing about the instrument, as the arching of both top and back was less pronounced than that of even the last of the Amatis.

It had the ornate Hill pegs, richly carved, that have not been made since the first years of this century, and were undoubtedly fitted at the time in the nineties when they made its case for Lady Tennant. The case, of the oblong shape, with an arched "roof" like an old-fashioned trunk, looked like a coffin for a little princess much too soon defunct, and was made of satinwood with borders of ebony and holly inlay, lined with light blue cut velvet, matching the blue velvet "baby blanket," white satin lined, beneath which the violin itself was cradled.

Taking the Strad out of that case for the first time, I remembered the caption of an old Percy Crosby cartoon of the *Skippy* strip: "It's so beautiful it makes you want to give somebody a sock in the eye."

But after looking at those sound holes, with their inimitable grace, I could only think of the sensation of recognition that floods a father at the first sight of a newborn son who is such a caricature of himself that he doesn't know whether to laugh or cry and, like old John Dodd, opts for a little of both.

I was itching to play it, of course, but had to reserve that thrill, not having reached the stage of shamelessness where I would venture to fiddle in the office except in the very early morning hours.

That thrill was worth waiting for. When I got it home and tried it, with my first Dodd bow, it almost seemed to play itself, at least by contrast to the degree of responsiveness I had ever felt in any fiddle before. And for the first time ever, I heard a tone come from a violin in my hands that didn't make me want to stop and put on a mute.

To most people of our day and place, time is reckoned in terms of B.C. and A.D. But surely to the better part of some five to six hundred people of this era, *their* time can only be expressed in

<

The Gudgeon in its Hill Case
Henry Wolf

69

The above illustration represents the house in the Haymarket known by the sign of the "Harp and Flute," in which Joseph Hill carried on business as a Violin Maker. It was next door to the Opera House, and was destroyed with the latter by fire, June 17, 1789.

SOLE GOLD MEDAL SOCIETY OF ARTS, 1885.   GOLD MEDAL INVENTIONS EXHIBITION

GOLD MEDAL PARIS UNIVERSAL EXHIBITION, 1889.

DIPLOME D'HONNEUR, BRUSSELS INTERNATIONAL EXHIBITION, 1897.

LATE VIOLIN & BOW MAKERS TO H.M. THE KING, H.M. THE KING OF ITALY, H.M. THE QUEEN OF HOLL

H.M. THE LATE KING EDWARD VII, H.M. THE LATE QUEEN VICTORIA, H.M. THE EX-QUEE

REGENT OF SPAIN, H.R.H. THE LATE DUKE OF EDINBURGH, AND

H.M. QUEEN ELIZABETH OF BELGIUM

WM. EBSWORTH HILL.
(Born 1817, died 1895.)

W. HENRY HILL.
(Born 1857, died 1927.)

ARTHUR F. HILL died 1939

ALFRED E. HILL died 1940

ALBERT P. HILL

DESMOND D. HILL

Workshops—LONDON AND HANWELL

ADDRESS FOR TELE
STRADIVARI, LO

140, NEW BOND STREET

LONDON, W. 18th May

WE certify that the *Violin in the possession*

Mr Max Moller of Amsterdam,

was made by *Antonio Stradivari of Cremona and bears a*

Description *The back, in two pieces, of wood marked by a curl*

width slanting slightly upwards from the joint; that

and head is cut on the slab and marked by a faint

The table of pine of medium width grain. The var

golden - brown colour. This violin is a characteristic

above period of the maker's work and, with the except

table which has been slightly repaired, is in an excelle

of preservation. *William E Hill & Sons*

A HILL CERTIFICATE   Charles Vaxer

70

nd .

dated 1672

edium

e sides

of a

rle of the

l the

tale

Certificate of

W. E. HILL & SONS,

HIS MAJESTY'S VIOLIN MAKERS.

1660, 17th Feb. "In ye morning came Mr. Hill, ye instrument maker, & I consulted with him about ye altering my lute & my viall.

1660, 5th March. "Early in ye morning Mr. Hill comes to string my theorbo, which we were about till past ten o'clock, with a great deal of pleasure. *Pepy's Diary*

1731, 6th March. In the Craftsman (or Country Journal), tickets for a Concert of Vocal & Instrumental Musick for the Benefit of James Jacobson, are announced for sale at Mr. Hill's Musick Shop in the Minories.

1742. In this year Joseph Hill was working with Peter Wamsley of "Ye Harp and Hautboy" in Piccadilly. A fellow apprentice was Benjamin Banks.

1756. In this year Joseph Hill moved his business from High Holborn (not then numbered) to Angel Court, Westminster, carrying it on at the sign of "Ye Violin."

1762. Joseph Hill removed his business to the Haymarket, and changed his sign from "Ye Violin" to "The Harp and Flute."

1784. William, Benjamin and Joseph Hill, sons of Joseph Hill, Jnr., violin-makers as well as musicians, took part in the Orchestra of the First Handel Commemoration at Westminster Abbey.

1808. Henry Hill in conjunction with Tibaldo Monzani, a Genoese by birth and flautist by profession, carried on business as Instrument and Music Sellers at 3 Old Bond Street, and, subsequently, 28 Regent Street.

1810. We think this was the year in which Henry Lockey Hill took patterns, still preserved by us, of a violoncello made by Stradivari, and sent over by Frederick William III, King of Prussia, to John Betts, of the Royal Exchange, to be sold in this country.

1848. Henry Hill (b. 1808, d. 1856) son of Henry Lockey Hill, played the solo viola-part in Berlioz's "Harold en Italie" on the occasion of its first performance in London.

1851. In this year the late Mr. W. E. Hill made a small violin, after the model of a dancing master's kit, on which H.R.H. The Duke of Edinburgh learned to play.

1885, 24th Jan. W. E. Hill & Sons were appointed the Experts in the Violin section of the South Kensington Loan Collection of that year.

terms of B.S. and A.S., before and after the acquisition of a Stradivari. To me the Glorious Twelfth can now only signify that
day in December, and not that other one in August, when the
grouse shooters in Scotland go berserk. And in my personal history 1966 has now become the most notable year since 1066.

Moennig—to whom I had confided that if he didn't want the
annoyance and trouble of having to come all the way to Sing
Sing to visit me, he would be obliged to wait until the end of the
next month for the balance due over and above the return of the
Cappa, which went back that same day—responded cheerily as
ever, reminding me that there is an expression, "broke but
happy," and pointing out, as its bright side, how much longer I
was going to be happy than broke.

Six weeks later, when I had become its owner in law as well as
in fact, he sent me its three certificates, his own and the two
prior ones from Max Möller of Amsterdam and W. E. Hill and
Sons of London.

The last is still the most prized piece of paper in the world of
stringed instruments, although the balance of power, as regards
the ownership of the world's remaining store of old-master fiddles, has long since shifted from the other side of the Atlantic to
ours. This is odd, since the handwritten Hill certificate doesn't
even carry pictures of the instrument in question, as the others
do. But the first thing anybody ever asks about a Strad, after its
date, is whether or not it has a Hill certificate. I had one, of
course, with the Cappa, so there was no longer the same interest
in going over the names and dates of the chronology of the house
of Hill, from 1660 onward, or the listings of medals won and
royal appointments enjoyed, which I had pored over when I
first got the Cappa, in the spring the year before.

Besides, there was no thrill left to begin to compare to that of
the first moment I had drawn a bow across its strings, and heard
that unique sound that David Sackson calls "the growl of a
Strad."

decided to call my Strad the Gudgeon, since there already was another one, well known and mentioned in all the Strad books of this century, called the Lady Tennant.

It might have been more gallant to call it the Erna Rubinstein, since she was its last famous player, but I had seen a picture of her, in one edition of the Grieg *Solvjeg's Song,* and her face wasn't one I warmed to at sight. She had the look of a spoiled brat, and while I had no idea, and no way of finding out, why she kept this Strad only ten years, still I was ready to hold that fact against her. Lady Charles Tennant, on the other hand, had kept it the better part of forty years, and left it better than she found it, in the sense that she endowed it with a worthy case; and since Max Möller acquired both her fiddles, the first of the year 1699 and this second one of 1672 at the same time, I was ready to assume that it was either death or incapacitation that made her part with them.

Besides, since it was out of the question to call it the Lady Tennant, because there was a later and greater one of the golden period that had preempted that name, I also felt that it would have been a bit presumptuous to call it the Erna Rubinstein, as she was a big player, which I could certainly never hope to be.

So I felt more comfortable calling it the Gudgeon, and I so identified it for Herbert Goodkind, for listing in his *Iconography of Antonio Stradivarius*, for which Moennig had already sent him photographs of it. Gudgeon was one of the two Georges in whose possession it had been before it reached the hands of either of its two later lady owners, and that made the name legitimate. Also, a gudgeon is a small fish, not much above the size of the average minnow, and since I don't aspire to attain even minnow stature as a player, but rather something on the order of the guppy, calling it the Gudgeon seemed not unduly pretentious.

Another reason for giving it a name with diminutive connotations was that in size, too, it was very small for a full-size Strad, being really what might be termed ladies' size. Strads average fourteen inches in body length, the inordinate length of the slenderized fiddles of the Long Period being compensated for by the number of times he made full-size fiddles under fourteen inches long, but this one is unusual in that it comes in under the $13\frac{3}{4}$-inch mark, which is normally considered the low end of the usual variance, from there up to $14\frac{1}{8}$ inches, for the full-size violin. True, it is just under the mark, being exactly 35 centimeters. There is only one other Strad of record as small as that, excluding children's violins like the famous L'Aiglon, and that is a Strad of 1684, listed in the Hill book, which is of the same length as this, but even slightly smaller in the width at its upper and lower bouts.

I assumed that the small size accounted in great part for its low price, as size is one of the factors taken into consideration, but, on the other hand, so is condition—that is, state of preservation, and this is almost as exceptionally good as the size is exceptionally small.

In any case, nobody could believe that in 1966 I had obtained a real Strad, undamaged and original in all its parts, and so attested by Hill, for anything like the $12,500 that I had paid for it. When I showed it to Luthier Rosenthal, on Fifth Avenue, he assured me he could get $25,000 for it, virtually sight unseen and about as quickly as picking up the phone and saying that it was in excellent condition and had a Hill certificate.

I asked Moennig for enlightenment. I knew that the early small *amatisé* Strads didn't command anything like the prices of those of the 1695–1720 period, and that the "hundred-thousand-dollar violins" were pretty well bunched around 1715. The Dolphin of the year 1714, for instance, known for distinguished owners from Count Cozio of Salabue in the late seventeen hundreds to Jascha Heifetz in the mid-nineteen hundreds, was reputed to have changed hands again at about that same time for a record $125,000.

As for my Gudgeon, I felt that I couldn't love it more, if it cost as little as twelve dollars and a half, or as much as that rumored record figure.

Moennig said there was no mystery about it. He had first acquired it right after the war when prices were momentarily depressed, had sold it immediately at a reasonable profit, reacquired it reasonably and had again sold it reasonably, and that it was as simple as that. But he did hope that none of the doubting Thomases I encountered would hope to acquire another Strad for $12,500, as they might wind up obliged to add an extra zero, particularly if the rate of inflation continued after 1967 the way it then appeared to be going.

Prices are relative, of course, and have always reflected "what the traffic will bear." In the first third of the eighteenth century the people around Cremona had an expression, "as rich as Stradivari," which served for that time and place much as the phrase "rich as Rockefeller" served for ours, two centuries later.

The price of a Stradivari in his own lifetime was high, in terms of the living standard of that day. The Hills estimated it as fourteen pounds, in translating the value of the ten gold Tuscan coins known as *gigliati* which was his normal price, except for elaborately inlaid instruments or court commissions. But that was in terms of the old British pound of the turn of the twentieth century, the five-dollar pound that would represent two of today's pounds since devaluation, and certainly no fewer than ten of today's pounds in terms of the purchasing power of the pound at the time the Hills wrote (1902). So if their estimate is thus updated to £140, or $336, it is easy to see that this was a princely sum. Even when the Hills wrote their book on Stradivari, a workman's wage was the proverbial "another day another dollar," and in the eighteenth century in rural Lombardy it was a fraction of that.

Stradivari made violins for his own account from 1664 to 1737, a working span of seventy-three years, and each took him about one hundred twenty hours to make, apart from the time he took varnishing them and letting them hang in the sun in the loft on his roof called the *seccadour*. Thus, while the printed estimates of his output have ranged from a low of one thousand to a high of three thousand, it seems sensible to split the difference and call it fifteen hundred. Hill estimates eleven hundred and Henley fourteen hundred, so perhaps it would be better to split that and settle for twelve hundred fifty.

Of that number, a bit better than half survive, according to the latest figures, which are Herbert Goodkind's: 630 violins, 15 violas, and 60 cellos.

Since Stradivari's life was his work, I think we can assume that he worked at least a ten-hour day, and that he could produce at the rate of sixteen violins or ten cellos per year.

Very little is known about him, and the portraits are of dubious authenticity. The most common one has him looking like Mozart, all ruffs and frills. The most satisfactory one is a word portrait, in which a contemporary pictured him, for me at least, more satisfactorily: he wore all white, a white leather apron and a white cap, linen in summer and wool in winter—what ineffable chic! Who could ask for more?

I began to love him only as I began to play one of his instruments, and by all accounts one of the first and the least of these. But now I found myself dreaming of him, and he became for a time at least the most important figure in my life.

The fiddle mania, which I had thought of as a long-dormant interest, until I tried to lay it away without flowers in *Toys of a Lifetime*, became a strong preoccupation immediately thereafter, and an obsession upon the advent of the Strad.

I realized that there are four sides to fiddling, and that, whereas my sudden crush on Stradivari (I say sudden because I had always been an Amati-Stainer man before that, i.e., an advocate of the old high arching) now led me to want to devour every word in print that I could find about him, it also made me more than ever uncomfortably aware that I had no business to be laying my unworthy hands on the least of his instruments.

I had been fiddling away shamelessly on the Kloz for months, and even on the Cappa, without feeling in any way apologetic toward those fiddles, beyond being ready to admit that they were both too good for me.

But now, in a clear-cut case of *noblesse oblige*, I suddenly found myself feeling ashamed that what I was doing, nights and weekends, I was doing to a Strad.

One day in January, just after getting back from a cruise, where atmospheric changes had caused the Kloz to come unglued along its right upper bout, I came into Rosenthal's at lunchtime, to leave the Kloz to be fixed, and I heard and saw a girl fiddling away like mad in the back room. She was playing double stops the way I wished I could play single strings, and I told Mrs. Rosenthal, who was waiting on me, that I thought the fiddling was terrific and wondered who it was. I was prepared to hear her say somebody like Erica Morini.

"Her name is Betty Ott," she said, "and she works for one of the women's magazines. You should have heard her six months ago.

She couldn't play from nothing, until Harry Shub took her on, and now she's ready for any symphony."

"Who's Harry Shub?"

"Oh, he's here. I mean, he's from Baltimore, and he still gives some lessons back there too, but he lives here now. He gives concerts. Here, take this." And she handed me a leaflet from a recital at Carnegie Hall the previous April.

"Of course, she looks thirty or less," I said, as Betty Ott went on fiddling in the back room, "and I'm rising sixty-three, but if he could do that for her in six months, maybe he could do something for me in two or three years."

"Here's his phone number," she said, writing it on the leaflet, "or, better still, if you want to come back for the Kloz tomorrow, he could come in and hear you, and you could talk about it."

I said that was great and started to leave, when old Mr. Rosenthal came in from the other back room, his workshop, and held out a topless fiddle, saying, "What do you think of this?"

He knew that I was a half-assed amateur fiddle fancier, and that I loved to be asked my opinion in all matters of authentification of fiddles and bows.

It was an old fiddle, yellow as my Kloz, and it bore the label of Giovanni Battista Gabrielli, Florence, 1750. Looking at the back, the pale varnish lambent as that of my Strad, and perhaps subconsciously influenced by what Moennig had said about the back of my Kloz, I said that the wood, as showing through that varnish, looked a lot older to me than any 1750, and turning it over and looking at the linings, I asked him if they weren't willow, which they looked like to me.

"They are," said Mr. Rosenthal with a conspirational grin, "and maybe you're thinking what I don't dare let myself think."

"That lightning strikes twice," I said, "and that you've got yourself another Stainer."

"That's what I'm thinking. You think so too?"

"Beyond a reasonable doubt," I said, "there were only two makers who lined their fiddles like that—Stainer, and, after him, Stradivari."

I had read that somewhere, and I've since learned it isn't true by a long shot, but he let it pass.

Some months before I had been in the shop with my batch of auction fiddles, to try to get him to make some minor adjustments on them, which he had reluctantly agreed to do, after pronouncing them all *dreck* (which I later learned was a word he was prone to apply to all fiddles from a provenance other than his own); and at that time he had shown me his latest find, the first genuine Stainer he had acquired in fifty years of looking for one.

I knew, simply because I'd read it somewhere sometime, that Gabrielli was the best of the Florentine makers, but that he only rarely deviated from the Stainer model, so it was not surprising that this topless "Stainer" should bear a Gabrielli label. But even so, I did honestly feel that the wood, both on the inside and outside views of the fiddle, did look appreciably older than the 1750 date on the label indicated.

"But what's a Stainer without a top?"

"Nothing," I agreed, "but you can copy the top from your other Stainer, and that way you'll have, if not two Stainers, at least a Stainer and three quarters."

He looked at me as if this thought had never occurred to him, and for all I know it hadn't.

Luthier Rosenthal was a wonderful violin and bow maker, who

had left Wurlitzer's in Cincinnati in 1918, before they had a New York branch, to strike out on his own in the big city. Though his success had come largely through dealings in old violins for such clients as Elman, Zimbalist, and Heifetz (and some were unkind enough to say that this side of his success had been largely his wife's, she being twice the trader he ever thought of being himself), he had impressed many knowledgeable people, Stokowski among them, with the quality of his own fiddles and fiddlesticks.

A Strad Without Its Top   *Luthier Rosenthal & Son*

<

A Stainer Without a Top
    Luthier Rosenthal & Son

He had made for me, when I first found out that Moennig wouldn't sell me the Dodd he had lent me, a tortoiseshell gold-mounted bow with the characteristic Hill & Sons whalebone wrapping that most old bows now bear, and ^{T} was using it at the office on the Kloz, along with the second of the two ivory-frogged Dodd bows. (I had broken up the pair after all, because the one with the ebony frog had a silver wrapping, like the first ivory-frogged Dodd that I kept at home with the Strad, and the gold-mounted, tortoiseshell bow that Rosenthal made me was actually a better match, with its whalebone wrapping, with the gold-mounted, ivory-frogged Dodd bow that I had kept at the office to use with the Kloz.)

As I left, Rosenthal said he thought he would take my advice, and make a new top for the Gabrielli, now known, if only to the two of us, as the second Stainer.

Overnight I kept hearing the sound of Betty Ott trying out one of Rosenthal's violins, and became hourly more determined to get Mr. Shub to take me on as a pupil.

When I played the reglued Kloz for him in the back room at Rosenthal's the next noon, his first expression was that of a man who has just been told that the chicken sandwich he is finishing was actually made of rattlesnake meat.

I spared him the necessity of saying anything by telling him that my last teacher, over fifty years before, had said that "it must be the way you were taught, because nobody could get that bad all by himself."

"No," said Mr. Shub, now swallowing as if he had just taken a test for the mumps, "it isn't as bad as that, it's just that it's so— well, what shall I say?—so chaotic."

"Well said," I told him, "I've been looking for a term to describe it to myself, and all I've thought of up 'til now is 'utterly unhousebroken.' "

He was a small dark man, with tremendous shoulder and chest

Luthier Rosenthal in 1966
The New York Times

Harry Shub
with his Guarnerius
Albert Kay

development, giving him the bodily aspect of an oarsman or a wrestler, but the size and intensity of his dark eyes gave his face an almost poetic expression, oddly at variance with his trim muscularity. I judged him to be about Rafael's age, mid-fortyish. He fixed me with those dark eyes, so intently that I felt the impulse to take a backward step, and said, "If you have the time to practice, even an hour a day, I see no reason you can't play, in a year or two, if not really well, at least acceptably. I mean acceptably by a musician's standards."

I said that was easy to promise, because between nights and weekends at home, and early mornings at the office, I was probably averaging better than an hour and a half a day, even without the incentive of lessons to practice for. But the thing I found almost impossible to promise, because my office time was subject to so many varying demands, was to keep any fixed lesson date each week with any hope of even reasonable regularity, unless it could be early in the morning.

"How early?" And I realized as he asked it that anything I considered early would sound to a musician like the middle of the night. So I suggested six-thirty, just to establish a point of discussion, and prepared to settle for a lot later than that.

"Good God, what time do you get up?"

I saw no point in shocking him with my actual four-forty, so I said instead that I got into town every morning on a five-thirty bus that was due in at the Port Authority terminal building on Eighth Avenue at Fortieth Street at five after six and actually made it most mornings by about ten after.

"If you could call me then," he offered, "when you first get in, maybe I could pull myself together enough to face you by seven."

And so it was agreed that I would come to his studio on Wednesday mornings at seven, giving him the benefit of as close to a full hour's advance warning of my arrival as I could manage. The choice of Wednesday was simply because that happened to be the next day, and I was very eager to get started.

His studio was at Seventy-second and Broadway, and on the IRT I could reach it from the bus terminal very quickly, in fact much too quickly, so I took to killing time in an all-night café on that corner, waiting for seven o'clock to strike. I usually had from thirty to forty minutes to wait, depending on my luck with the subway trains and/or whether I happened to catch a Seventh Avenue Express or Local.

Getting back down from his studio to my office on Madison between 51st and 52nd streets was much more involved, taking two subway changes, so I settled for a Broadway bus, that came down from Riverside and was jammed by the time it reached 72nd Street, but nearly empty when it went down Fifth Avenue below Fifty-seventh. Getting on encumbered with both briefcase and fiddle case earned me such dirty looks from the women on that crowded and comparatively infrequent Number Five bus, laden though they were themselves with huge handbags and shopping bags, that after the first Wednesday I brought a fiddle in to leave in Mr. Shub's studio.

I chose the Little Red, the Mori Costa that I had acquired at auction for ninety dollars, and the first time Mr. Shub heard it, and tried it himself, he found it hard to believe that it hadn't cost at least several times that amount. It was Jane's favorite among my fiddles (for reasons still known only to herself she had taken an instant dislike to the Strad), and when I told her my teacher liked it that predisposed her favorably toward him, whatever she might think of my subsequent progress.

After hearing me play my one Handel Sonata through from start to finish, Mr. Shub decided not to attempt to reshape my handling of that one, the sixth in E Major, but to put me through the others, either as quickly or as slowly as I showed I could absorb them.

Getting out an edition containing all six, he started me on the third, rather than the fourth in D Major, generally regarded as the great one, because he felt the third would be easier for me rhythmically because it is for the most part so much more "catchy."

That was the first and the last time, to the best of my recollection, that he ever showed the least sign of any tender mercies for my inadequacies as a performer, as his plan right from the start seemed to be to throw the book at me, exposing me to as much of the standard repertory as I could conceivably be expected to cope with, no matter how ineffectually.

Before I was halfway through the Handel sonatas he had me started on the Vivaldi Concerto in A Minor, Op. 3 No. 6, and from then on there was never a time when he didn't have me entangled in some bête noire that was so far over my head as to make everything else that he had me working on seem easy by contrast.

The tactic was utterly unorthodox, and at variance with his method with all his other pupils. But I was the only one with a forty-nine-year gap between lessons, and obviously such an unusual case called for a complete departure from the usual treatment.

Within the year he had me tangling with the thickets of such difficult things as the Saint-Saëns *Introduction and Rondo Capriccioso*, the Vitali *Chaconne*, the Corelli *La Folia*, the first of the Bach *Sonatas and Partitas for Violin Alone*, and even—forgive me, Felix—the Mendelssohn Concerto.

These peaks made sonatas by Handel, Mozart, and even Brahms, and five Mozart concertos, seem relatively negotiable foothills by contrast.

It might sound crazy, but it seemed to work, and within a matter of weeks I was beginning to make the Strad sound with more than an occasional and coincidental resemblance to the way it should sound in the hands of a violinist as opposed to those of a collector.

Up to now, I realized, my only serious approach to the violin had always been that of the collector, whether actual or armchair, and this was a very lopsided way of going about paying one's full measure of respect to this most complex of all instruments.

A while back, without going into it, I mentioned the four sides of fiddling, and they are, of course, making the violin, composing for it, playing it, and collecting it. This last is, of course, the only one into which no active element of artistry enters, since it is the one that considers the object not as an instrument but as a work of art.

There have been outstanding exponents of all four of these aspects of the violin over the roughly four centuries of its history, and in each there stands, and probably will forever, one unrivaled name. They are Stradivarius, Mozart, Paganini, and last—and, at first blush, least—Tarisio. Yet, but for him, quite possibly a great number of the Cremonese masterpieces that survive today might never have been preserved, if he had not gone around Italy in the twenties, thirties, and forties of the last century gathering them up, like a peddler, in a bag on his back.

Three of the four are Italian, which is not surprising, as the violin was born in Italy.

Born is the right word, too, rather than "invented," because it really grew up in the family of viols, and has such siblings as the viola and the cello. And while it must be classed as an inanimate object, because it is man-made, rather than born of woman, it is more truly a work of art than a mere artifact, and it transcends the category of simple objects of utility in that, in its highest reaches of development, its unique examples defy duplication, whether by man or by machine.

This is one of the reasons it has such a powerful mystique, because, though it is well within the grasp of modern science to do such unheard-of things as put a man on the moon, it is not yet within our power, nor is it very likely now that it ever will be, to match the varnish of a Stradivari, nor yet to duplicate its tone.

We have learned to do such once-inconceivable things, in the course of our current explosions of knowledge and technology, as to take frescoes off the walls on which they were painted centuries ago, tour them over continents, and put them back again, but we still cannot, either through chemical analysis or mechanical duplication, recreate a single masterpiece of the Cremonese violin maker's art.

I know that I have no gift whatever for two of these four aspects of the compleat fiddler. It is well over fifty years since I last tried either to make a violin or to write anything for it. I was taking harmony lessons from Mrs. Loomis in Grand Rapids when I wrote a piece that turned out, by sheer inadvertence, to be in two keys at once. Although the course had been paid for in advance she refused, after that, to go on with the lessons.

"Not unless your name is Leo Ornstein, and you know that you're in two keys at once and, right or wrong, you at least know why you're doing it. None of that applies to you."

So she finished out the term with little lectures on Italian art, with particular stress on Giotto and Fra Angelico, on the grounds that she knew I could at least see what she was talking about, something that she despaired of ever making me do as long as she went on talking about what could and should occur within the bounds of the five staves of a musical clef.

As for the fiddle's two other faces, now that I had a Strad my collecting thirst was at least momentarily slaked. I could feel for those Parisians who always turned up their noses at the notion of travel, on the perfectly logical basis of "Why travel, when you're already there?" After all, when you have a Strad, where else is there to go?

On the other hand, the more I played it the more I realized what a long way I still had to go, before I could begin to feel that I really played it well.

Hence, for at least a month, I thought of nothing else.

SIX

Once the acquisitive itch has got me, in whatever field of collecting I have strayed or wandered into, I am of those who, with Oscar Wilde, can resist everything but temptation.

It came in mid-March '67, about a month after I had begun taking lessons, in the form of a phone call from little old Mr. Rosenthal, that gentle man, who seemed so old only because he was already so sick, suggesting that I stop in at the shop to see what he had done with "our" Stainer.

Having just finished paying for the Strad a matter of some six weeks or so before, I had certainly not thought of myself as a very good prospect for the purchase of another fiddle, no matter what or by whom. But the way in which he had seemed to include me in what had happened to this particular fiddle made me feel, even if it was no more than a manner of speaking, that it would be pretty impolite not to stop in and have a look at it.

I hadn't been a bit sure, when he showed it to me without a top and with the Gabrielli label in it, that it was a Stainer, and had said so more or less at his prompting after I had remarked on the willow linings. It was not very logical, after all, that a genuine Stainer would be masquerading under a Gabrielli label. Since the Florentine Gabrielli was a follower of Stainer, using his model after a lapse of about a hundred years, it would have seemed much more plausible if a genuine Gabrielli had sailed under the false colors of the much more famous maker, and had been provided with a Stainer label.

But after making that guess, based on no more than a hunch and the fact that the linings were willow, I had tried in vain to find what I thought I had remembered reading somewhere, that only Stainer and Stradivari used willow linings.

I couldn't find it in any of the dozen fiddle books where I thought it might have been, and began to wonder if I had dreamed it. In the Hill book I found that only Stradivari used willow both for the linings and the corner blocks, in contrast to the practice of the Amatis of combining pine blocks with willow linings, but nowhere could I find again that elusive sentence that bracketed Stainer and Stradivari in this one unique characteristic.

In Stradivari's own lifetime, and particularly in his youth, Stainer and Amati violins commanded prices four and five times as high as those he obtained for his. Stainers and Amatis were in fact favored by the leading violinists of Europe throughout the first three quarters of the eighteenth century, and it was only during the following fifty years that the ascendance of Stradivari, begun by Viotti in the seventeen eighties in Paris and later when he lived in England, was completed. The Del Gesù vogue was even later in starting, beginning with Paganini in the eighteen twenties.

But I did find, in Sandys and Forster's 1864 volume, *The History of the Violin,* the statement that "many years ago" 1500 acres of land was paid for a Stainer violin—land worth a dollar an acre at the time—but Sandys and Forster gave it the topper for violin prices of all time by adding "we understand that a large part of the city of Pittsburgh has been built on them."

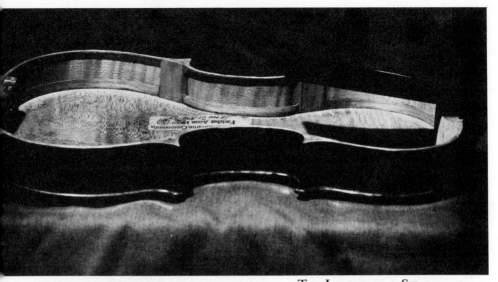

THE LININGS OF A STRAD
Luthier Rosenthal & Son

THE LININGS OF A STAINER
Luthier Rosenthal & Son

THE STAINER WITH A
ROSENTHAL TOP
Henry Wolf

I copied out the passage in Sandys and Forster and sent it to Mr. Rosenthal, to bolster his already high opinion of the value and scarcity of genuine Stainers.

When I went in to look at his handiwork on "our" Stainer, ex-Gabrielli, I was very much impressed with what he had done. Nobody but an expert would have been able to say, on picking up this fiddle and looking at it from every angle, just which part was old and which was new. In this penultimate year of his life, Luthier Rosenthal was convinced that he had at last penetrated the long-lost secret of the old Italian varnish. Stainer alone, among non-Italian makers, had it, lending credibility to the other-

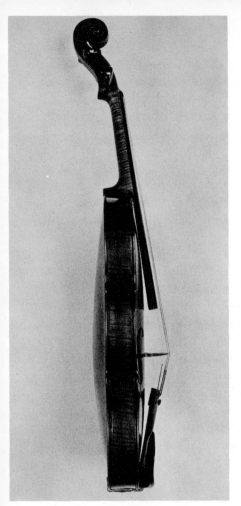

wise unsubstantiated legend that he worked some years in Cremona. Mr. Rosenthal hadn't rediscovered the long-lost art of making the varnish that was common to Cremona fiddles up to the last quarter of the eighteenth century, and never since duplicated, but he had duplicated the top of the intact Stainer so skillfully that, looking at them side by side, you would have found it hard to say with any degree of certainty which one was old and which one was new.

For one thing, he had used some very old wood, that he had hoarded for more than forty years against just such a contingency as this. Also, he had managed to get in the look of a couple of very slight and extremely well-repaired cracks.

Picking them up and playing them, one after the other and back and forth, there was a difference, but so slight as to be barely discernible, especially to the listener, although perhaps a bit more readily apparent to the player. The "new" fiddle, that is, the one with the new top, seemed just a trifle less responsive, and just a shade more strident. But the difference, in both respects, was so minute that if somebody had taken them both into the next room and kept switching from one to the other, it would have been impossible to remain absolutely sure, each time that happened, just which was which.

One thing about the new one I didn't like. Mr. Rosenthal had taken out the old Gabrielli label and inserted a very phony-looking Stainer label. I say phony-looking perhaps because I knew it was faked, but in any case I think I would have recognized the label, even if I hadn't seen the fiddle before with the Gabrielli label in it, because it was very obviously taken from the 1659 Stainer label that seems to turn up in virtually every fiddle book published between the sixties and the nineties of the last century. He had photostated it, bleached the photostat, and then, without bothering to change the 1659 date, had carefully retraced the outline of Stainer's handwritten letters. I thought it was redolent of fraud, and hated to see it put into an otherwise worthy instrument.

Whether he had removed or simply covered up the old Gabrielli label I don't know, and as he has since died I probably never will, but I would have preferred to see him insert his own label, with a notation to the effect that he had made a new top for this old fiddle and that it was his opinion that the rest of it was the work of Stainer in the seventeenth century rather than of Gabrielli in the eighteenth, as the label indicated, and leaving the old label in.

He was of course doing only what violin makers have done for centuries, at least as far back as Nicolo Amati's lifetime. The Hill book and several others report the suit brought by the violinist Tomaso Vitali in 1685, the year after Amati's death, seeking restitution of the sum of twelve pistoles, because he had discovered that the violin purporting to be the work of Nicolo Amati, and for which he had paid sixteen pistoles, had, beneath the Amati label, that of Francesco Rugeri, an Amati pupil, whose violins were known to be worth, like any other new violins at the time, only four pistoles.

Rugeri, known as *il Per,* has long since become a maker esteemed in his own right. Beethoven had one of his fiddles and was proud of it. But he was by no means alone in the practice of lessening sales resistance by putting his master's label either over or in place of his own. Cappa must have done the same thing and even more often, because the Hill brothers, Henry, Arthur, and Alfred, in their book on Stradivari in 1902, said they could recall only one instance in which Cappa had used his own label instead of that of Amati, which made me think they must have been mindful of certifying my Cappa for Miss Warren of Deal in 1888. Even in that case, though the label plainly read 1683, they certified the fiddle only as "period of 1680."

Obviously, to the one playing any violin, it can't possibly make any difference which particular piece of paper is pasted inside, nor for that matter whose scroll adorns the peg box, which is the only portion of the fiddle's head that is essential to its function as an instrument. But the contribution of either the top or the back, and especially the former, is vital to the tone. This is reflected in the enormous difference in the prices collectors are prepared to pay for the work of given makers, if either of these two vital parts is determined not to be original, as contrasted to the relatively slight difference made by the presence or absence of the original scroll.

Rosenthal explained, for example, that he couldn't hope to get more than forty-five hundred for the Stainer with the new top, or less than a fourth of the price that he was virtually certain of getting for the Stainer whose top he had duplicated. To the collector, three-quarters of a Stainer or a Strad is like three-quarters of a dog or a horse to the fancier of the thoroughbreds of those species.

Although my own collecting avidity was in momentary eclipse

because of my very recently revived playing interest, occasioned by the acquisition of the Strad, still I did entertain the thought that it might be nice to have even a semi-Stainer around the office, to use in place of the Kloz.

But I knew the Kloz would be the stumbling block in any deal I might attempt to make for the Stainer, as nobody had ever been very enthusiastic about appraising it for much more than half the thousand dollars that had been paid for it over thirty years before, and Rosenthal had himself said that he doubted that he could get more than five hundred for it.

The Strad had so recently left me "happy but broke" that I felt more fear than hope of acceptance when I finally ventured to offer twenty-five hundred and the Kloz for the Stainer.

Rosenthal seemed disappointed that I couldn't make a more serious offer than that, and I sensed his disappointment with relief.

But I had not reckoned on the resourcefulness of Mrs. Rosenthal. The matter had not been reopened in more than a week, and I'm pretty sure Mr. Rosenthal would have left it alone, but one day she called me to ask if I would send over the Kloz.

I said I would, but wondered why, since I knew that Rosenthal knew it better than I did myself, having, only weeks before, reglued it where it had come open.

"Oh, sure, my husband knows your violin very well, but there's this other fellow, that I'm trying to get a painting from, who doesn't know it at all. He wants fifteen hundred dollars for the painting, but I figured maybe I could get him to take the Kloz instead, and then everybody'd be happy."

I figured Mrs. Rosenthal's power of persuasion would have to be enormous, since she must have known her husband's dubious opinion of the value of my Kloz, if she expected a man to part with a fifteen-hundred-dollar painting for a maybe five-hundred-dollar fiddle, unless of course the value of the painting was as *maybe* as that of the violin.

MRS. LUTHIER ROSENTHAL   *Luthier Rosenthal & Son*

Also I wondered why, with a vaultful of fiddles, the Rosenthals should find the only key to their dilemma in a violin that wasn't theirs. I didn't have long to wonder, however, as Mrs. Rosenthal called back the next day with the unlikely news that the man was enchanted with my Kloz, she adored her painting, and her husband was delighted that I was going to get the Stainer after all, because he had done the work on it with me in mind and was in fact going to say so on its certificate. Now, if they could just have my check for twenty-five hundred, the Stainer would be mine, and I could join the daisy chain, where happiness was rampant.

Mathematics has never been my long suit, but I did figure out that the price of the Stainer had just come down, though by just how much I still wasn't sure, since the actual cash involved in my original rather reluctant offer still seemed to be the same.

Let's see. If my Kloz was worth the thousand dollars my wife had paid for it, when I got it from her in 1936 as a sort of combined birthday and Christmas present, then I was giving only thirty-five hundred for the Stainer that Mr. Rosenthal had priced at forty-five hundred. But if the painting was fifteen hundred, and was being bought with my Kloz, then the cash consideration would mean that the price of the Stainer was now four thousand, or down five hundred.

The only figure that didn't seem very fluid in the whole transaction was the five thousand at which Luthier Rosenthal appraised the new fiddle for insurance purposes. Since insurance companies are accustomed to insuring rare old instruments, at the time of their purchase, for ten per cent more than was paid for them, then that would indicate that the price of the Stainer had advanced to $4,550, pushed up by the painting purchased by the might of my Kloz. I never saw the Kloz again, but, instead, the Stainer came back to me from Rosenthal's housed in the scruffy, worn, old crocodile case that had already been venerable when I got it with the Kloz in it, back in 1936. It has so long been a component of the shabby-genteel tone of my office that it would have been missed.

In it came also the certificate in which, after attesting that the violin was in most parts original with the famous Austrian craftsman, Jacobus Stainer, Rosenthal went on to describe the instrument as follows:

"It has a two-piece back of flamed curly maple. The sides and scroll, as well as the interior is original by the above master including the varnish which is the usual golden, brown color. The preservation of these parts is excellent. The top, which was made by the undersigned, was a most challenging work ever attempted by the undersigned. The success of this operation speaks for itself. It required not only skill but a great deal of courage in which Mr. Gingrich supplied both good suggestions and advice. Most important, the tone quality is as fine as any concert instrument."

Nobody even got a new case out of the transaction, and I could only assume that the man who had the painting, since he presumably delivered it uncased, got the Kloz the same way. Or, as Rafael said of the Guarneri he got from Hill & Sons in London, they didn't give him so much as an old brown paper bag.

On the exchange of punts, so to speak, I gave up an old Kloz

Luthier Rosenthal is here shown holding in his left hand the Soil Strad, and in his right his copy of it.

Luthier Rosenthal & Son

with a putative back by Duiffoprugcar and wound up with a putative Stainer, with a new belly by Rosenthal.

As a conversation piece, the Kloz was the better of the two, with the endless debatability of its having what amounted, in violin terms, to a prehistoric back, though I must concede that in regard to tone Rosenthal was right.

Luthier Rosenthal had not much longer to live after that. The ravages of cancer were soon thereafter evident, and he died within two years, at just past seventy-seven. That is no great age nowadays, and especially not for a violin maker, of whom the greatest lived and worked the longest: Stradivari until he was ninety-three, Amati, eighty-eight, and even John Dodd of Kew, with all that purl, until he was eighty-seven.

In the whole *histoire* of "our" Stainer, it's the one thing I regret.

SEVEN

ith a better fiddle to play, and new music to work on,
thanks to Harry Shub's practice of rationing the Mozart like candy to a child, and not letting me have another sonata
until I had crash-stormed my way through something else more
difficult, I now found myself fiddling longer than ever each
morning in the office.

But I was still hesitant about playing beyond eight o'clock, as
people tend to begin showing up in the halls after that hour,
though for the most part they turn out to be messengers just
coming through for pickups and deliveries. Even so, unless playing with a heavy mute, which tends to diminish the clarity and
the enjoyment proportionately, I hated to go on perpetrating—
despite closed doors—that peculiarly penetrating din that only
the unaccompanied violin can inflict upon involuntary listeners.

Besides, by eight o'clock my conscience would start demanding
that I look at some of the papers that pile up on my desk and on
my coffee table every night after I leave. Most of them can be

disposed of long before the arrival of any such leisurely convenience as a modern secretary, simply by reading and initialing,
or by scribbling on them either horseback decisions or buck-
passing comments.

In other words, it suddenly occurred to me that there were things
I could just as well do while listening, even if I did have to stop
fiddling to do them.

Obviously, what I needed now was a tape recorder. At a fishing
lunch I had seen a man with one, and noticed, as I never had before, that at some time in the not-too-distant past they had become as portable as a camera or a transistor radio, with
shoulder-slung carrying case, and that, thanks to the convenience
of cassettes, they had become almost as easy to use. I copied
down the name and model number, Norelco 150, and got one
the same day.

In the past I had had the so-called portable tape recorders. They
were portable only in the sense that they were not actually
nailed to the floor, and were of the reel-to-reel type, which, even
to a fly fisherman, inured to the exigencies of what Jane always
called a niggling-piggling pastime, were infuriating to use with
their constant need to be respooled and rethreaded. The re-
threading, particularly, I had always regarded as of a malignancy
that made the worst crotchets of sprocket-jumping movie film
seem benign.

But now with these cassettes, playing at the slow speed of one
and seven-eighths feet per second, as opposed to the old seven-
and-a-half-foot speed, I found I could in effect double my morning fiddling time, because cassettes play and record forty-five
minutes to a side. So with one simple flip-over of a cassette, and
no rewinding, I could, from six-thirty to eight, record everything I played, and then, from eight until nine-thirty, play it
back, with the volume turned down, or even silently, thanks to
earphones—blessedly available as an optional extra. In the latter
half of this solitary time I normally spend in the office every
morning anyway, I could not only get some work done but at

the same time learn more, in terms of what mistakes to concentrate on and what phrases and passages to rework, than I ever could while trying to play and listen simultaneously.

True, the fidelity left something to be desired, but so did my intonation, which made me feel that we deserved each other, the cassette and I. Besides, accounting for a good part of my ever-present feelings of inferiority about my fiddling, I found that nothing sounded half so bad when played back as I had thought it sounded while attempting to muddle through it.

Up to now I had had no other counterbalance to Janie's constant belittling than my teacher's weekly comments, and they weren't always uplifting to my morale, either. Now, like a monkey with a mirror, I suddenly found that I could have more fun with my fiddle than I had ever dreamed.

Thanks to the earphones, which permit turning the volume to zero and still hearing perfectly, while at the same time cutting down the drain on the batteries, I could even go through my practice sessions on subways, buses, and airplanes, with the score in my hand, watching and listening for mistakes and means of improvement. Also I found this latter practice an invaluable shortcut to memorizing the music.

Soon I found that I felt just as undressed without a tape recorder around my neck as I've felt all my adult life without a briefcase. Stewardesses always think it's a transistor radio and ask me to turn it off, until I tell them what it is. People on the street tend to think it's a camera, except at World Series time, when everybody's always asking me the score.

Weekends I found that by recording and re-recording (as with most tape, it erases automatically as it records) to correct mistakes and smooth out rough passages, I could put my best foot forward for my teacher at the next lesson, and he too seemed to find the device a convenience and a shortcut, as it enabled him quickly to determine which weak points needed his concentrated attention or correcting.

But backing up to re-record, or even to play back a given passage to see how it sounds, is a great nuisance because it means you must unplug the recording microphone in two places before you can rewind back to the desired spot in the tape to play it back or to record over it. So, after the first weekend of this, I got another machine, so I could simply lift out the cassette from the one that was set up for recording and play it back on the other one that was ready for rewind and playback. And, shortly thereafter, so I could do the same thing at the office without looking like a beast of burden carrying two machines to and fro, I got a third.

I wish I could say they're as efficient as they are convenient, but they aren't. I keep thinking there must be some better brand or model, but none of them seems to be well enough made to stand the punishment of such constant use as I give them.

In theory, my need for three is dictated only by my desire to be set up for convenient recording and playback both at the office and at home. In practice, it turns out to be imposed by the need to have two of these machines in functioning shape somewhere while the third is back at Norelco for repairs.

Nor is the repair service ideal. I have had the infuriating experience of waiting three weeks for the return of a nonfunctioning machine, only to be told that "the factory couldn't find anything wrong with it," when the simple test of trying to play it would have told any fool but a factory expert that the damn thing just didn't play.

As of now, one of my three plays slightly sharp—about three-quarters of a tone high. An even half, or even full, tone too high might lend a sort of specious brilliance that my playing admittedly lacks, but not quite a full tone too high and just enough more than a half makes it come out even more sour always than I only sometimes play it in. Another one plays back fine, but fails to erase as it records, with the result that I can make myself sound like a Chinese duo, trio, or even large ensemble, depending purely on how many successive times I try to record on that one, except with virgin tape. A fourth eccentricity, which has so far fortunately affected only the first of the three above-mentioned machines, is a tendency for the sound to conk out, except at very infrequent intervals. Normally, you can hear the playback at anywhere above 2 on the volume dial that has its degrees of loudness gauged by markings of 1 to 9. For nine minutes out of ten, on the playback of this machine, you can barely hear it at all at any point below 9, and then, when the sound does occasionally go on full strength, it blasts you through a brick wall. Obviously, this machine is now really functioning only as a rewinding device, just to save the annoyance and nuisance of unplugging the one I'm recording on, since it neither records at proper volume nor plays back at proper pitch.

Bad as they are, they're wonderful for me, and I wouldn't give one of them up for anything if I couldn't get another. Thanks to them, I practice twice as efficiently and memorize at least three times faster. (Just lately, I've discovered the greater sophistication of the Japanese tape recorders. I have a Concord, which will rewind and play back, during a recording session, without the necessity of removing any of the recording controls. In fact, you can record with the microphone still kept in the carrying case. It costs more than the Norelco, and its tone is actually not as rich, but the logistics of recording on it are simplicity itself. So, ideally, I record on the Concord, and then, if I want to play the tape for anybody else, I do it on whichever Norelco happens to be both handy and in the mood to function.)

Since their advent the pattern of my lessons has changed, to the obverse of that of my morning fiddling sessions in the office, where I record all my fiddling first, and then play back while I start to cope with things on my desk. In my lessons, on the other hand, we now start by listening to the recording of whatever tasks had been set for the week, and Mr. Shub listens, usually score in hand, and makes constant comment, and an occasional notation on the scores, to serve as reminders to him of which mistakes to concentrate on when we actually begin to play. My playing is then largely confined to doing, over and over until I get it right, whatever I may have done wrong, and his playing, at this corrective stage of a lesson, is a demonstration, whenever needed, of just how those particular passages should be treated. Then, when we break new ground, with a piece of music that I have never played before, he plays it through for me, and has me try only the hard spots where he anticipates my having the most trouble.

Often I surprise him, and come back a week later with a recording in which the new tune's hard spots are negotiated with fair fluency and passable correctness, but the ostensibly easy portions are mangled almost beyond recognition, due either to a basic misapprehension of their rhythmic pattern—places where there is some syncopation, for instance, and I land on the wrong beat— or to an overconfidence that makes me careless in the intonation or slovenly in the execution of the passages that I think are too easy to study.

It is exactly like the way an uneducated person will write a letter. All the big words are correctly spelled, because he has to look them up, whereas all the easy words, like "which" and "their" and "you're" are consistently misspelled.

Mr. Shub's comments on listening to the recordings made on the preceding Saturday and Sunday mornings, when I have plenty of time to erase and re-record again and again until every passage goes as smoothly as I can make it go, cover a wide range, from many "goods" and even an occasional "bravo," as I surpass his expectation on the hard parts, to an anguished "ouch" and a frequent "there you loused it up" and "this must be worked out" on the parts that had been assumed to be easy enough to require no hard practice and deep study.

Now and then he will say, "I would keep this tape," so I lay that particular one away, after dating it and noting which fiddle was used on it, and every so often, when I play back old tapes, I will be discouraged by the feeling that some of the old ones are better than I can do today on the same tunes, even though I may have reworked them several times in the interim. This has happened most often on cruises (where I have a lot more time on my hands than I ever have ashore, and can play over the old things that I normally wouldn't want to take the time for), and whenever it does I have a strong impulse to jump overboard.

Mr. Shub tells me I am wrong to let things like that discourage me, and that if he had any way of hearing tapes now of things he had played at the age of ten, that he still plays today, he might well feel the same way. He also reminds me that we hear things in different moods, from one time to another, just as we may not feel exactly twice alike when we play, so it's not surprising that a thing can sound better—or worse—to us at one time than at another.

Music is, of course, the most subjective of the arts, or was at any rate until the phonograph came along to enable us to preserve it like canned goods. Before that, you could say that music didn't exist except as it was born again, each time it was performed. Today the electronic media homogenize the arts, and even those ephemeral forms, music and the dance, can be summoned back to life again, out of the limbo of performances past, at the push of a button.

At the opposite pole from music and the dance, disallowing this new factor that confers imperishability on performances of both of them, are sculpture and architecture, the two art forms that are the most obviously independent of their creators and practitioners, once they have been constructed. In between are books and plays, which can both be said to live in the mind's eye of the reader, even though only the former are meant to be read and the latter to be acted. Paintings, too, can survive in books and prints, though the originals be removed for one cause or another; but it must be conceded that they survive thus only in diminished effectiveness and stature.

But music exists to a greater degree in what it does to you, than can be said of any of the other arts. Except for your hearing of it, it doesn't exist, as books and paintings, buildings and sculpture can be said to exist, as background or decor, whether you pay any attention to their meaning in themselves or not. In canned form, of course, music now exists too, as background, in elevators, between announcements in airports, as "atmosphere" in otherwise silent scenes in movies—in this form it exists, where the evident assumption is that little or no attention will be paid to it.

But when we are making music ourselves, music exists only because and as long as we are making it, because we will it into being, and it lasts only as long as our interest does, and until we turn to do something else. So it is completely subjective, as even finger painting is not. Almost everything else leaves some residue, to be picked up and put away.

The same is of course not at all true of the means of making it. A piano exists, in many if not most homes that have a piano, simply to serve as a setting for bric-a-brac and photographs, and to raise a table lamp to the level of a floor lamp. Even worse befalls some violins, reduced to serving as "planters" in which to grow green things.

But while we are using a musical instrument for its prime purpose, unless we are doing it professionally, our motivation is for the most part self-serving and ego centered. That's apt to be as true when we're doing it with others as when we're doing it alone. The Amateur Chamber Music Players are surely not brought together by any desire to make music for the joy of their entire community, but only for one another.

I often wonder, as I'm fiddling in a hotel room between appointments, or listening with rapt attention to one of my tapes on a plane between cities, whether what I'm doing could not be classed as one of the worst forms of narcissism. What, next to playing the third Mozart Concerto in G, with the Franko cadenzas, could be more egocentric than listening to oneself playing it, over and over, with neither company nor accompaniment?

Maybe this accounts for the slightly pejorative ring of the word "fiddle," except of course as used affectionately by fiddlers. To other people, surely, no aim to praise is implicit in such phrases

NARCISSUS AT THE MUSIC RACK   *Henry Wolf*

as "fiddling around," and as for "Fiddlesticks!" it is certainly
tantamount to "Rubbish!"

To us who worship the likes of Tourte and Dodd and Peccate
and Voirin, such use of a word as that given to "fiddlesticks"
should presumably bring a worse reaction than the use of the
word "nigger" occasions to all concerned, but I've never known
a fiddle maniac to rise to it with any special vigor.

What will bring a rise out of any fiddler is the sight of a new fiddle. They look at them the way other men eye girls. The big
difference is that the older the fiddle the livelier the interest. A
new fiddle must do for the morale of a fiddler what a new hat is
reputed to do for that of a woman.

In my own case, I had supposed that my newly intensified interest in playing the violin, induced by my guilt feelings about touching the Strad, would tend to diminish my interest in collecting. The Stainer was of course a slight setback to that supposition. But I had rationalized that two ways, first on the grounds that I had more or less inadvertently allowed myself to be made an accessory to that venture by old Mr. Rosenthal, and second that I had more or less "needed" a better fiddle for the office.

But one morning in May of '67, when the Stainer had been in my hands less than two months and I had put it down and begun playing back what I had taped, and while looking over my desk to see what might require attention, I noticed a copy of a new issue of *The World of Strings*, Moennig's occasional catalog–house organ.

There were undoubtedly things there that required more attention than that, and it may even be that there still are, because I seldom have time to get below the upper strata of accumulation, but this did just happen to be on top.

I noticed again that the fiddle offerings lacked price indications, as indeed they had in the last few issues, and was slightly disappointed by it, as I imagined a lot of its readers would enjoy, as I did, using it as a means of keeping an eye on the market in old violins. Even when you haven't the least notion of buying anything, it's always nice to know what this or that make may be bringing, as prices rise and fashions change, in this or in any other field.

Still, I supposed this kind of interest meant that Moennig would get more mail, as it was plainly and prominently stated that prices would be given on request.

I was struck by the utter absence of Amatis in this issue, as I couldn't remember when there hadn't been at least one, and they were what I always looked for first. But one page was devoted to the pictures and descriptions of three Guarneri specimens, an Andrea, one by his son Joseph known as *filius Andreae*, and one by *his* son, the Joseph known as Del Gesù.

The first two made my mouth water, as I had long harbored an aim so secret that I hardly acknowledged it to myself, of some day owning one of the Andreas—either Amati or Guarneri— or even, though I imagined it might cost more, a Joseph *filius Andreae*. So I dropped Moennig a note saying that I would be interested in learning their prices, at his convenience, as I wasn't in a position to think of another fiddle—or at least to do more than think about another—for some time to come.

The only surprise in his answer was the price of the Andrea, which was nineteen thousand dollars—fifteen hundred higher than the *filius*. The Del Gesù was thirty thousand, not high at all, since his violins are the only ones to enjoy parity with Strads.

When I expressed to Moennig this surprise at the price of the Andrea, he agreed that it was unusually high, but that it was the finest Andrea that he knew of, and that in the Hill certificate that it bore they said that in their opinion much of the instrument was the work of Andrea's son Joseph. So I told him I would have to forget about the Andrea and go on hoping that lightning might strike twice, and that some day an early Amati, either by Andrea or his sons, Antonius and Hieronymus, would come along as advantageously as the early Strad which I cherished.

By return mail he told me that he had just obtained the opportunity to acquire an outstanding A. & H. Amati, Cremona 1610, that he had been after for a long, long time and that now suddenly, for some reason or other that he didn't know, had to be sold before the end of May, so he was leaving for Europe right away, and he enjoined me to keep my fingers crossed.

Wow. Joe Wechsberg's had been 1608, and I had always been verdant over it. Fingers firmly crossed, I was off on another flight of anticipation—that giddiest of the collector's joys.

EIGHT

hile I was waiting to hear again from Moennig, after he had gone off to Europe in May of '67, hoping to return with the A. & H. Amati violin about which he had written me, I further whetted my appetite for an Amati by reading everything about them that I could find. This is not easy, as there is no book about this first family of violin makers of Cremona. There are books about the Guarneri family and about the Guadagninis, and one about Maggini, whose author, Lady Margaret Huggins, in the foreword to the Hill book on Stradivari, just after the turn of the century, pointed out that her book on Maggini was but one of a projected series of lives of great violin makers, and that many lives, "those of the Amati especially," must be written. But that was almost seventy years ago, and the book of the Amati remains to be written, although one of the most active of the producers of the constantly growing literature concerned with the world of the violin is named, ironically in this circumstance, the Amati Publishing Company.

Andrea Amati, born about 1535, was certainly by a few years, at least, the senior of the Brescian Gasparo da Salò, so long thought of as the father of the violin, and whether or not Amati, or anybody else, can ever at this late date be proved conclusively to have been the first maker of true violins, there can be no doubt that his name, as carried on by his two sons, Antonio and Hieronymus, and the latter's son Nicolo, remained throughout the next century and a half the greatest in fiddledom. It was only some years after Nicolo Amati's death in 1684, at the age of eighty-eight, that the Amati name and fame were at last transcended, and then only by the two names that had become known to the violin world after apprenticeship in his shop—Stradivari and Guarneri. As the grandson of one Andrea, and the master of another, Nicolo Amati stood halfway, in a span of almost two hundred years, between the beginning of the violin and its highest peak of development, as represented by the first violins of Andrea Amati and the last ones of Del Gesù, the grandson of Andrea Guarneri.

The Brothers Amati, Antonius and Hieronymus, worked together in their father's shop and took it over after his death. They labeled their best violins jointly, and while each did sign some individually, they seemed to work better together than apart. The exact date of Antonio's death has never been established. Hieronymus, the younger of the two, was taken by the plague, along with his wife and two daughters, in 1630. His son Nicolo, then 34, was spared, or the subsequent development of the violin might have been very different. For without him, and his great fame, to whom might Stradivari have been taken for his apprenticeship? Since Stradivari, in his inlaid violins and in his designs for patterned fingerboards, tailpieces, bridges, and the frog of one bow in particular, showed himself to be greatly gifted both as draftsman and carver, it is conceivable that he might have made a name for himself in some entirely different application of his talents. In fact, Baruzzi in *La Casa Nuziale* advances quite convincingly the argument that in his early years, and for a few years after his marriage in 1667 particularly, the paucity of Stradivari's production of stringed instruments is to be accounted for by the fact that he could make more money as a carver and inlayer than as a violin maker, and that his few violins of the years before 1680 were really spare-time productions. This is in contradiction to the long-accepted theory that he was kept so busy in those years working for his master, Nicolo Amati, that he was able to make and sell very few instruments of his own.

Many of these questions will of course never be resolved, but will be debated interminably in the talk of fiddle fanciers. As a means of courting sleep they serve much better than sheep counting.

My own head was buzzing with bits and pieces of miscellaneous information about the Amatis, sought out as a means of easing my impatience while awaiting not only Moennig's return from Europe but also the A. & H. Amati that he might be bringing back with him, to send me for trial.

When he came back with it, in mid-June, he sent me photostats of its certificate and details of its history as supplied by Pierre Vidoudez of Geneva, through whom he had acquired it. This was enough to send me right back to my books again, as it was unexpectedly complicated and involved.

It turned out that this violin by A. & H. Amati, Cremona 1618 (and not 1610 as Moennig had remembered it), was enlarged by Nicolas Lupot in Paris in the early eighteen hundreds, some time shortly after he set up shop there in 1796, had become a part of the stock, so to speak, of the Lupot establishment, and had been in and out of the shop often over the next hundred and fifty years. In the last century it had belonged for some time to the celebrated French violinist and composer Henri Vieuxtemps, and his case for it, of black lacquer encrusted overall with mother-of-pearl ornamentation, and an elaborately embroidered satin-lined silk throw carrying his initials HV, had ever since, according to Vidoudez, been "piously preserved." On the outer case, of leather, there was an inscription, in Vieuxtemps's hand, now no longer legible but still distinguishable.

Lupot, known as the French Stradivarius, was violin maker to the Paris conservatory, and one of his violins was annually awarded there as a prize, a distinction that was passed on and

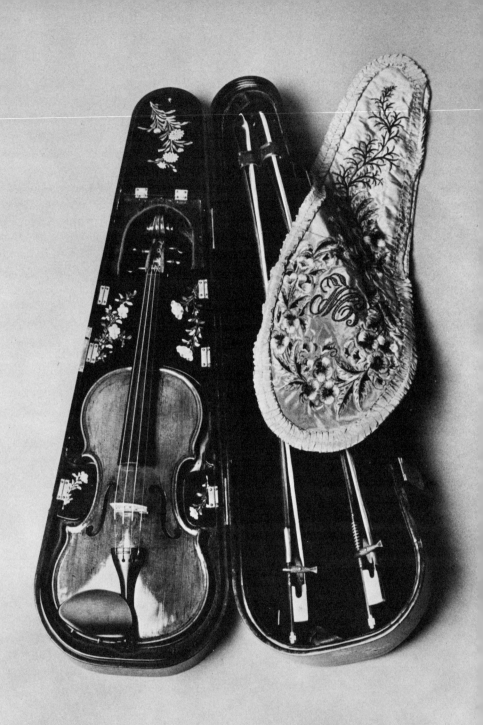

enjoyed in succession by each of his successors in the firm ever since, from Gand, through Gand & Bernardel, to Albert Caressa and Emile Français, the last two of whom had issued certificates for this violin in 1937 and 1950, respectively.

As was not too surprising, seeing that Moennig had acquired this fiddle from Pierre Vidoudez in Geneva, it had belonged, from 1937 on, to a near neighbor of mine, though I didn't know it at the time, throughout the four years I lived in Switzerland. It was a part of the collection of Gustave Huguenin of Vevey-Corseaux, just a few hundred paces down the *corniche* from where I sat in the shadow of Chexbres. Huguenin was a knowledgeable collector who had, among other fiddles, a Strad, a Del Gesù, a Sanctus Seraphin that had once belonged to Ole Bull, and a whole quartet of Jacobus Stainers that he had left to the Music College of Winterthur, his home town.

The thing I found fascinating about this fiddle, when Moennig finally sent it to me for trial over the long weekend of the Fourth of July, 1967, aside from its tawny yellow varnish and tiger-striped back, and the double rows of purfling, one of which had been added by Lupot when he enlarged it, so skillfully that you couldn't tell whose row of purfling was which, was that I seemed to see in it, at first glance, the prototype of the Long Strad pattern. I had always thought that the Strad *allongé*, which marked Stradivari's widest deviation from the classic shape of the Grand Pattern Amati, was a unique departure in violin body design, quite apart from the question of arching, and that once he departed from it, to return to the less attentuated shape of the violins of his golden period, this swanlike fiddle shape had never been seen before or since. But, except for being higher arched than even my Strad *amatisé*, this violin, made twenty-six years before he was born, could well have served as his model for the Long Strad. Lupot, in enlarging it, had not changed its original contours at all, adding about three-eighths of an inch all around, to bring its body length to 35.5 centimeters, or a just

<

THE VIEUXTEMPS A. & H. AMATI
Henry Wolf

slightly scant fourteen inches (about 13 $\frac{31}{32}$ inches). Its width at the upper and lower bouts was still scant, as against those of the Strads before 1680, and more nearly proportionate to the narrowness of those of the Long model.

Its tone took me by complete surprise, because, while it seemed at first blush to have the typical Amati softness, I found that on bearing down the least bit it had a bell-like, almost trumpet-loud,

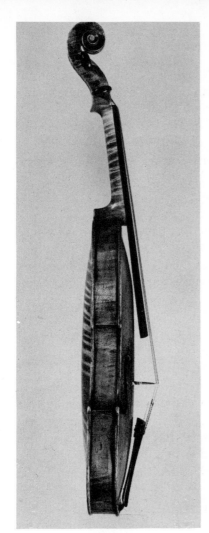

ANTONIUS & HIERONYMUS AMATI, 1618
Wm. Moennig & Son

intensity. In fact, with vigorous bowing, it seemed to develop twice the decibel strength of my Strad. In short my Strad, *plus royaliste que le roi,* seemed much more Amati-like than this early Amati. Of course there was the difference of a half-centimeter more in length, and about the same in all the other dimensions of breadth, to account for this difference, plus the considerably higher arching of the Amati, though I had never thought of this last as adding to the tone, but, in fact, as diminishing it. The sound holes were just as long as those in the Strad, but slightly more perpendicular, and rounder—in other words, more Amati-like. In fact, except for being longer, they looked more like those of the Stainer than of the Strad.

I played the three fiddles back and forth and, so to speak, against each other for the three days of the long weekend, and reached the conclusion that the Amati had the biggest tone of the three, less piercing perhaps than the Stainer's, but certainly more robust than that of the Strad.

Violin tone is a subjective thing, of course, to at least some extent. I think we hear partly with our eyes, and I kept wondering whether or not I would have flunked a blindfold test, on distinguishing those three fiddles every time, if I had been playing them in a totally darkened room, and had had somebody take one away and hand me another, and switch the order on me, say, every three minutes for an hour. But one thing I have since decided is that part of the question of subjectivity in deciding matters of tone lies in the fact that first impressions cannot be trusted.

Once I got the Amati and the Stainer away from the Strad, by taking the first to the office and leaving the second at my teacher's studio, my impressions of the three fiddles changed almost as often as I played them, when I had only the recollection of the sound of the other two, no matter which one I happened to be playing.

I have since heard, as well as heard of, several tests, of different fiddles being played against each other, and I wouldn't trust the results of any of them. As time went on, I found myself liking the Strad more and more, and both of the others less and less. How could that factor ever be allowed for, in any test conducted at any one given time and place?

As it happened, the long weekend served only to complete my first infatuation with the Amati, and by the end of that time I would have ranked the Strad second and the Stainer a pretty bad third.

After a couple of years of playing them, however, I would have put the Strad ahead, by a mile, and the Stainer ahead of the Amati. Not that they had changed, but I had.

Long before the two weeks of the trial period had passed, in fact by the eleventh of July, the Amati was mine. I had found that the only satisfactory way to tell Moennig the answer to the question implied in sending it to me was by the simple three-word verdict, "Enclosed find check." Not that this was as easy as it sounds— I had done some fast scurrying to cover the quick five thousand that it took.

But its shipping case did not go back empty. The Amati had been brought to me as I sat working at the New York Public Library on Friday afternoon before the long Fourth of July weekend, and I had opened its case within eyeshot of one of my cellmates in the room where I was holed up working on a book project.

His name is Ferdinand Lundberg, and all we had ever had occasion to discuss, up to that moment, was pipes and tobacco mixtures. But when I opened the case to look at the Amati, he said "May I?" and leaned over from his cubicle next to mine.

Another fiddler. Lapsed, or resigned, or anyway "ex-," but a fiddler never loses the eye for a new fiddle, however long it has been since he's touched one.

He offered to bring his in for me to look at, and did so, the day after the long weekend.

It was an ugly old thing, of the Maggini model, cherry-red on back and sides, with the belly black as sin or as those oxheart cherries that are of a red so dark as to be almost black. It was monstrous, looking almost like a viola, compared to my fiddles.

This, together with the nearly sooty aspect of its top, gave it an almost grotesque, gargoyle-like appearance. At first glance I found this repellent, and only after repeated studying did it begin to exude a rather raffish charm. It was in an old Wurlitzer canvas-covered oblong leather case, and had the companionship of an obviously pretty good bow, gold-mounted with ebony frog.

Lundberg said he had had the whole outfit since 1934, and hadn't touched the fiddle for some years. He was in fact ready to sell it, as he couldn't invest the time that he knew it would take to put his fiddling back into any sort of decent shape. He was working very hard, and had been for several years, on a big elaboration of a small study of "the two hundred families" with which he had attracted considerable attention back in the mid-thirties, and knew he would not want to take up again a hobby that he had always found much too time-consuming. (The book he was working on, and which appeared the next year, was *The Rich and the Super Rich.*)

Although he had paid only a couple of hundred dollars for the fiddle well over thirty years before, he had "always understood" that it was a genuine Maggini, though he had never had any sort of certificate or other documentation concerning it.

One glance inside was sufficient to show that the label, at least, was not genuine, as Maggini was misspelled, lacking one "g," but even more damning, it was dated, as Brescian violins of the time of Maggini and his master, Gasparo da Salò, never were. Dating the labels was a Cremonese practice, begun by old Andrea Amati in the fifteen sixties, but very seldom done in Brescia for the next hundred years.

The fiddle appeared sufficiently dark and dirty and beat up to account for every one of the three-hundred-fifty-odd years that the date on the label ascribed to it; but turning it over and studying it from every angle, I began to doubt that it was more than about a third of its purported age.

It's hard to tell why wood, especially as seen through varnish,

"The Monster" (after G. P. Maggini)

Henry Wolf

should give even the roughest indication of its age, but somehow it does, and you needn't have seen very many authentic old violins before you begin to be able to distinguish the really old from the merely elderly.

But he who would be his own expert in a field that juts with such tricky angles as this one is an even bigger fool than he who would be his own lawyer, and deserves himself as client. I told Lundberg that, to me, this looked like a nineteenth-century violin, whether Italian or not I couldn't even begin to guess, but that I would guess that its value could still be reckoned in the hundreds rather than in the thousands, despite the inflation that we both knew had occurred since even the "baloney dollar" days when he bought it.

But since the library is just across the street and down a block from Rosenthal's Fifth Avenue shop, I suggested that he take it to old Luthier and get his expert opinion of its worth. At the same time I warned him of Rosenthal's tendency to dismiss as *dreck* almost any fiddle short of a Strad or Del Gesù of any other provenance than his own.

But I was still not prepared for the word that Lundberg brought back, not quite twenty minutes later, from his visit up the street:

"He didn't say the fiddle was *dreck*—that's what he called the bow. He said the violin was a monstrosity, and that if I didn't want to play it I should use it to grow plants in."

Lundberg was so visibly shaken by Rosenthal's rude dismissal of his long-cherished possession that I felt sorry for him. At that time I didn't know anybody at Rembert Wurlitzer, or I'd have sent him right back out again with it, around the corner and west on Forty-second Street, following the principle of telling a rider who has just been thrown to remount and ride again. But then I remembered that, back at the office, the trunk that had brought the Amati from Moennig by REA Protective Signature Service was still standing empty, so I volunteered to take the fiddle home that night, and encase it in that trunk early the next morning at the office, where I spent the time anyway each day, waiting for the library to open at nine.

Cleaning it up that night, with some of Rosenthal's Violin Varnish Cleaner and Polisher, I saw a difference in its appearance that was almost as revelatory as that occasioned by the bath given Eliza Doolittle at Professor Higgins' orders. Revealed, for one thing, was the name "Fergus," written as if with a diamond in the varnish on its back, over near the middle of the right-hand lower bout. This was intriguing, because I had looked at the fiddle a number of times without noticing it, and neither had Lundberg, as it turned out when I asked him about it the next day. It was of course more suggestive of some previous ownership than as a clue to its origin, since owners write their names or initial, or put their seals, even on violins of great value—something they would never dream of doing with any other precious object, whereas makers, except of pianos, have generally had enough respect for their instruments to put their names inside, out of sight.

Looking at the Amati, however, I began to wonder whether it might be an exception to this rule, because on the button, that little promontory at the top of a violin's back outlining the base of its neck, there were the initials P. L., incised rather more artistically than the usual inept penknife scratchings of owners.

Knowing that Nicolas Lupot had a brother, François, who was as great a master of the bow as he was of the violin, I tried to make the P read as an F, but the letters were a little too well carved to encourage this confusion.

So I wrote Moennig, at the same time that I wrote him about Lundberg's purported Maggini, asking him his opinion of the significance of these initials on the button of the Amati.

I knew that Moennig, whether or not he agreed with my own horseback opinion that the Maggini was a nineteenth-century copy, would at least be polite about it, and not add insult to the injury given Lundberg's feelings by Rosenthal.

123

I had played the fiddle, the night I had it home, and had been astonished by its small sweet voice, as surprising in a fiddle of that size as the high small voices of such big men as Jack Dempsey and the late William Randolph Hearst. Any doubt I might have harbored about whether it might actually be, as Lundberg believed, a really old Brescian violin was set to rest immediately. It had none of that dark tone, sombre and ever so slightly tinged with hollowness, that I had always associated with Brescian fiddles. At that time, though I have since played several, I had actually only once ever held a real Maggini in my hands. It had belonged to my old connoisseur friend Frank Stewart in Grand Rapids when I was a kid in knee pants. I had never forgotten either its rich deep tone or its pale tan color—almost beige-light, though of a more saffron tinge. Its rows of double purfling, looped gracefully at the top and bottom of the back, must have been black and white, as all purfling is, but in my mind's eye they still "read" brown against that yellow of the old varnish.

Well-preserved old violins, always cared for as objects of beauty and value, are still bright after hundreds of years. Most of the Strads and Amatis and even some Gasparo da Salòs, ranging in age from two hundred fifty to almost four hundred years, look newer at first glance, and a lot better maintained, than most people's two- to four-year-old cars. That's why it's so hard to explain, even to one's own satisfaction, why it's so easy to tell the real old ones from their modern counterparts, even when the latter have been "aged."

For instance, at first glance, I might not know which part of my Stainer had been replaced, but I'm sure that on a careful looking-over from every angle, despite the very skillful job of putting in what look like well-repaired cracks and a darkening of the varnish around the bridge and across the middle, that makes Rosenthal's new top for it look remarkably compatible, I feel pretty sure that, without being told, I could tell, not perhaps that the top was only some three years old, against the three hundred and some of the rest of it, but at least that the rest was old and that that one part wasn't.

In any event, in this one instance I apparently could tell, when I guessed nineteenth century as opposed to early seventeenth for the age of Lundberg's fiddle.

Moennig, true to my expectation of his "Sweet William" behavior, paid Lundberg the courtesy of calling him at home in Westchester to discuss the fiddle and bow, and while he agreed with my hunch that it was a nineteenth-century copy, he went further and said that it was not Italian but French (a distinction a violin maker would know how to make but that I obviously wouldn't), and that in his opinion it was probably the work of Mathieu. He said it was difficult to pinpoint many of these Magginis copies, for there were literally hundreds made by lesser makers, among which only those made by the better makers such as Vuillaume were readily recognizable. Charles de Bériot started something of a vogue for Magginis (because he played one) second only to the Del Gesù craze started earlier in the century by the fame of Paganini's red Cannon.

As for the bow, on which I hadn't hazarded a guess, beyond the commonsense deduction that nobody would have wasted gold mountings on a stick that was a piece of junk, Moennig said it was early French, perhaps slightly older than the fiddle, and of the school of Adam. He added that the frog was not French, and was probably made in England.

He said that, as bow prices go compared to those of violins, the bow was more valuable than the fiddle, though neither was of any real value, but that the bow could conceivably fetch two hundred to two hundred fifty dollars, while it would be hard to get more than two hundred fifty or at the most three hundred dollars for the violin itself.

Lundberg, having made up his mind to sell them, was willing to let them go at the lower of those figures, but Moennig said that neither was up to the minimum level of the class of offerings on which he liked to concentrate his efforts, and he wouldn't undertake to sell them, even on consignment.

The upshot was that I offered to take them off Lundberg's hands at the minimum figures mentioned, although in contrast to

Moennig's findings I liked the fiddle much better than the bow, which felt like a club after my Dodds.

While my need for either fiddle or bow was anything but evident, I had much less cause for compunction about diluting my "collection" with copies than Moennig had evinced, since the foundation of mine, now that the Kloz was gone, remained the four mongrel fiddles and bows picked up at auction, all even more innocent of any sort of documentation than the Maggini-Mathieu fiddle and the school of Adam bow.

And considered as an exemplar, even though not original, of one of the basic schools of violin design, this Maggini model was actually a better stand-in for the real thing than any of the four auction fiddles in their respective representations of the main features of the characteristic patterns of the Stainer, Amati, Stradivari, and Guarneri makes. These latter could serve at best as mere *étalage*, like those pasteboard mock-ups of real merchandise that had to serve as space fillers in so many central European merchants' display windows in the months after the end of the war in Europe, until, through currency reform and renewed production, real merchandise offerings could be diverted from the black market and brought back into normal channels of display and sales.

Now that I had the 1618 Amati, even that dubious service was no longer required of the four auction fiddles and I soon found that I was no longer taking either the Marconcini or the anonymous Stainer model out of their cases, even to look at, though I still found I had some fun playing the other two now and then.

Some added documentation on the A. & H. Amati came along when Moennig forwarded a letter he had received from Pierre Vidoudez in Geneva, to whom he had relayed my question about the initials P. L. carved so artfully on its button. Vidoudez, too, thought that the initials were the gratuitous lily-gilding of some owner, and of no very likely coincidence with Lupot, either François or any other. He said that he thought it was most probable that they had been put on sometime early in the last century, after the violin was enlarged by Lupot and before the time of Vieuxtemps. He had often seen such initials on violins, even on very expensive ones, such as the Strad marked with R. K. (meaning Rodolphe Kreutzer of Kreutzer Sonata fame), and an Amati that he sold to Queen Elizabeth of Belgium and which bore the signature Ch. de Bériot, and others for which he could never find any similar significance.

(One obvious exception, of course, is the branding of some of the finest Strads with the initials P. S. in the "throat" below the G-string peg in the pegbox—the brand by which Paolo Stradivari marked those violins that were left in his father's workshop.)

Vidoudez added that Gustave Huguenin had lost all the papers for all his violins during the war, and had caused duplicate certificates to be issued wherever possible, as in the Emile Français certification of this A. & H. Amati of 1618, the ex-Vieuxtemps, which served in 1950 simply to confirm and replace the earlier lost certificate of 1937 issued by his predecessor, Albert Caressa. When Mr. Huguenin parted with the Amati, as well as with most of the other instruments of his collection, except the quartet of Stainers which he bequeathed to the Winterthur College of Music, he sold it to a lady who, by the time she in turn brought it to Vidoudez in Geneva, no longer had any idea of what might have happened to that piece of paper she had got with it.

This didn't matter as much in this instance as it might have in others, as Vidoudez had known that particular Amati even before 1937, during the time he had himself worked for Caressa in Paris, and could easily have certified it, together with the otherwise lost details of its enlargement by Lupot and its ownership by Vieuxtemps. But the original certificate was of course to be preferred, coming as it did in direct line from Lupot to the Caressa and Français firm, and it occurred to him to check with Mr. Huguenin's son, to see if by chance (having once before had the experience of losing a certificate) the precaution had been taken of having this second one of 1950 photocopied at the time it was obtained to replace the lost one of 1937. With typical, if tardy, application of characteristic Swiss prudence, this had indeed been done, and thus Vidoudez, upon acquiring this Amati, had been able to furnish Moennig with at least a copy of the document that was supposed to accompany it.

To me the chief interest in all this, quite apart from my original and natural curiosity as to who might have carved his initials on a Cremona fiddle that was made two years before the Pilgrims landed at Plymouth Rock, was that I thus learned that I had, once again, acquired a lady's violin.

True, I didn't know even as much about her as I knew about Lady Tennant and Erna Rubinstein, who had preceded me in courting the affections of the Strad, but at least I could conclude that her careless handling of the Amati's certificate was good enough indication that there wasn't much more worth knowing about her.

About Lady Tennant herself I have never been able to find out anything except that her husband's name was Charles and her London address was Grosvenor Square; but about Erna Rubinstein I have since learned that she was Hungarian, born about 1906, and a pupil of Hubay at the Budapest conservatory, and that after playing as a child prodigy with orchestras in Budapest and Vienna she toured with success in Germany, Czechoslovakia, the Scandinavian countries, and Holland, making her New York debut with the Philharmonic in 1921. While still in her teens she was well enough known internationally to be included in the Biographical Dictionary of Violinists in the 1924 edition of Alberto Bachmann's *An Encyclopedia of the Violin*. It was in this work that I learned—in addition to these details, and saw again the picture that I didn't much like—all I had previously known of her: she had "a splendid technique and a remarkable tone."

The picture of Erna Rubinstein, on the cover of her concert edition of the Grieg *Solvjeg's Song*, came to me from Ferdinand Lundberg, who decided, as long as he was getting rid of his fiddle and bow, to get rid of his music as well, and began bringing it in to me at the library by the bale, so that for the next two weeks I was laden like a burro, going home on the bus every night with two big briefcases filled.

PIERRE VIDOUDEZ AT HIS BOW BIN
Wm. Moennig & Son

THE PICTURE OF ERNA RUBINSTEIN
Charles Vaxer

What I especially treasured, in addition to the standard repertory items like concertos and sonatas that I knew I'd be working through like a termite with Harry Shub, was a virtually complete run of all the Kreisler items, the greater part of which are now out of print. No more agreeably violinistic music has ever been written or arrayed than the many Kreisler compositions and transcriptions, and the fact that there is now too little call for them to keep them in print, particularly in this age of facsimile when it's so easy to get virtually anything copied, is an ironic commentary on today's tastes.

This little treasury of Kreisler music, alone comprising some seventy-odd items, of which about half were things I could not otherwise have obtained, turned my folly in buying Lundberg's fiddle and bow into a rare investment, and would in themselves have constituted a very generous "makeweight," when he chose to regard them as part and parcel of the sale; but when added to all the others it meant that he was quite literally giving me back more money, in music, than I had paid him for the violin and the bow, to say nothing of the handsome and serviceable leather case with its canvas cover, which were also thrown in. I was very glad, the next summer, when his book turned out to be a best seller, for it seemed a rare proof, in these otherwise cynicism-inducing times, that there still are instances where "virtue will triumph," and that nice guys don't necessarily always finish last.

Just the same, though this little added detour to the purchase of the Amati made me feel good, I still resolved after two fiddle purchases in not much more than as many days, to declare a moratorium on fiddles and bows, and to spend instead more time and attention on the playing of these instruments of which I now had more than the proverbial one for every day of the week, and to concentrate on the attempt to master some measurable portion of all this music that I was now hip deep in.

For the rest of '67 and I hoped for all of '68, I was determined to buy no more than the occasional string I would need to keep eight fiddles in playing shape, and the occasional piece of music that I might not be able to find in my suddenly sizable private stock.

NINE

Since it would be foolish and futile for a man who is well into his sixties to think of playing the violin for any other aim than his own amusement, there is really no way to explain why, after the spring of '67 when I had resumed lessons following a lapse of forty-nine years, I began concentrating on its study like a kid cramming through a crash course of preparation for a crucially important exam.

Since nobody cared in the least, except perhaps my teacher, whether I could or couldn't play a given passage in a given work, the only way I can account for the intensity of effort with which I now attacked my studies is to compare it to a sort of self-imposed purgatory, in expiation for my sin in having frittered away a small fortune on eight fiddles and nine bows in little more than a year.

That the whole amount, roughly twenty thousand dollars, would constitute any sort of fortune in the eyes of anybody but the citizens of underdeveloped countries did not lessen the impact of the realization that it had been spent, as my Pennsylvania Dutch forebears would have said, "for pretty" and hence was crazy foolishness.

I would have settled, I thought at this point, for the ability to pick up any one of the fiddles, including the Strad, and perform on it even one piece well enough that it could not be deemed, in all objectivity and fairness, an insult to the instrument.

The one piece of any pretension whatsoever that I knew was the Handel Sonata Number Six in E Major, and I realized with astonished shame that after all my years of sawing away at it I didn't even know what E Major meant. It was only after Lundberg taught me a memory device that I could look at a piece of music and tell that it was, for instance, E Major if it had four sharps in the signature of the clef at the beginning of each line.

I could tell by reciting the key sentence that Lundberg told me:

"Go Down And Empty Barrels Fully."

From left to right the initial letter of each word indicates the number of sharps in the major mode, the number ascending in accordance with the order of the words, as G for one sharp, D for two sharps, to F♯ for six sharps.

In reverse order, the same sentence gives the number of flats, as one for F to six for G.

But Lundberg never told me any similar sentence that would do the same duty for the minor mode, and I still don't know what C Sharp Minor, for instance, may mean, except that I think it's something that pianists have to worry about (when they encounter the Chopin waltz of that description) and that, up to now at least, I don't.

Speaking of pianists brings back to mind the story they used to tell of the February night in 1917 when Jascha Heifetz made his New York debut. Mischa Elman and Leopold Godowsky were sitting in the same box, and about halfway toward intermission-time Elman asked Godowsky if he didn't think it was uncomfortably warm in the hall that night, and Godowsky answered, "Not for pianists."

A February date in 1917, as I remember, was the first of a series of dates marked by my teacher of those days in my copy of the six Handel sonatas for violin and piano, only the sixth of which was marked up. It had a succession of dates, from February to October of that year, indicating my teacher's expectations of my progress through successively dated portions of its four pages. The last time I remembered seeing that particular copy of the violin part, still bearing the dates penciled in by Sherman Tuller of Grand Rapids, now long dead, was in the house in Switzerland, sometime in 1945 or 1946; and I suppose that means that it is still to be found somewhere in one of the many footlockers, filled with household effects, that made the round trip to Switzerland between 1945 and 1949. Most of them have never been opened since. I imagine other markings on those pages indicated fingerings simplified for my sake, and bowings broken up, wherever too many notes were tied together for me to handle in one stroke. But the only other notation I recall distinctly, apart from the succession of dates, was the single phrase scrawled across the top of the first page, already faint in 1945, where my teacher had written, "Play *in* the strings."

Today, more than five decades later, I am still trying to live up to the implications of that simple admonition, and still not finding it easy. Dr. Samuel Johnson is imperishably on record as being of the opinion that there is nothing more difficult than to play the violin. He cited other things that any man can do, if not well then at least well enough, at the first try, and, as I remember, they even included shoeing a horse, which is something I wouldn't care to try, but he concluded with, "Hand him a violin and he can do nothing."

Fitness for other things in no way presupposes any natural aptitude for the violin, as witness a story I remember reading in the Fall 1960 issue of Moennig's *The World of Strings*, in which a contemporary was quoted as saying that "Patrick Henry was the worst fiddler in the colonies, excepting Tom Jefferson."

Jefferson said that music was the favorite passion of his soul, and by other accounts he was deemed at least passable as a violinist. Even so, that must have made his fiddling the least of his distinctions, with which we all think of him today as having been super-endowed. But one of them is that he was one of the earliest owners of a Cremona violin in this country, so, though we cannot know whether or not he was a good fiddler, we can at least know that he had a good fiddle.

The relationship between the two is only coincidental. Rafael Druian can pick up the worst of my fiddles and bring out of it a better sound than I can draw from the best, and so can my teacher, Harry Shub.

My only consolation, after several years of hard work, is that today I can myself draw a richer tone from the lowliest of my four auction fiddles, the tubby and nameless Stainer model, even with the shoddy Japanese "Vuillaume" bow, than I could draw from the Strad itself, with the peerless first of my Dodd bows. I found this out not long ago, quite by accident, when, on a morning that I found my office bedecked with painters' tarpaulins, the only fiddle I could reach and snake out from under the white canvas turned out to be the least esteemed of my violins. The fact that I could now make it sound like something, at any rate compared to what it sounded like the last time I tried it, a couple of years back, was a headier thrill than I could have imagined.

I took it as a token of progress, in my long campaign to become, if never a really good fiddler, still a better one than I ever was. It served too as something of a check on the reaction of my only constant audience, as expressed in Janie's repeated remark, "You're better than you were, but you're still dreadful."

That last, of course, I am entitled to ignore, since it is well established that a man's wife can testify neither for nor against him. Nor do I take too much stock in what my teacher says, giving it about the same literal credence that players accord the remarks of the coach in the locker room between halves. Mr. Shub, like another Rockne, is obviously trying to stimulate me to ever greater effort, and I allow for that in everything he says, knowing that he must feel the need to exert a countervailing pressure against the natural tendency of the student to become discouraged.

He started me, rather than with my old Sonata Number Six that I knew by heart, on the other Handel sonatas, Numbers Three and Five, and then the great one, Number Four, in D Major.

This was on the wise premise that it would be easier to get me started right, on something I didn't know, than to try to straighten me out on something I'd been doing all wrong for years.

And lest I go stale on too much Handel, he threw in after the first couple of Handel sonatas, and for simultaneous study while I was tackling the great D Major Handel Fourth Sonata, the Vivaldi Concerto in A Minor, Op. 3, No. 6.

And before I had rounded out the Handel Sonata volume with Numbers One and Two, he had thrown the Mozart Strassburg Concerto at me, the Fourth, in D Major, complete with Joachim cadenzas. This was at first like so much sound in the gears, and the resemblance of the sound to music must have been only vague. It revealed that, anywhere above the first three positions, my fingers ran only from fright, and that anywhere above the normal range of the human soprano voice, I didn't really know which notes I was reaching for.

Scale exercises, such as Lundberg had given me in abundance, would undoubtedly have done a faster job of straightening me out in this respect, but having elected the unorthodox course of trying to teach me to fiddle the way you might teach a boy to swim, by the simple means of throwing him in the river where it's over his head so he'll have to swim, he stuck to it, and before long, upper-register passages that had at first been hideously out of tune, all the way through, began to be succeeded by similar passages where the occasional excruciating blooper only served to point up the fact that almost all the rest was pretty well in tune.

To reduce this to a truism, it was a simple demonstration of the basic soundness of the bromide that nothing succeeds like success. Perhaps also applicable was the principle of the French proverb to the effect that appetite comes in eating, because it seemed to be true: the one way to get to play these things that at first blush appeared to be away over my head was to play them until I could play them—in other words, let the technique evolve through the playing the way the appetite develops in the eating.

I know that if you had simply shown me the scores of some of these things and asked me if I could play them I'd have said, not in a thousand years. Even the Vivaldi, relatively simple though it was, seemed an impenetrable forest of black notes when I first looked at it, outside the campus music store in Ann Arbor where I picked it up, for my next lesson with Mr. Shub the following Wednesday. If I'd been in New York at the time I'd have grabbed the nearest phone to ask him if I had indeed got the right concerto, as it seemed so preposterous to think I could play anything that looked so complicated and such a far cry from, for instance, *Simple Confession*. But as it was, since I was between appointments to which I was being convoyed by a student guide, I let it go, and by the time I got back to New York I had forgotten about it.

At my lesson, the following Wednesday, playing along behind Mr. Shub the way a tenderfoot follows a guide, I found that indeed there was a fairly simple path through the forest, between the trees, so to speak, that had appeared to be such a formidable black mass.

It was a little like the time I got John Hennessy, the Davis Cup tennis player, to give me a game of singles at the Saddle and Cycle

Club in Chicago, as part of the deal in buying a piece from him for our then new magazine. It was the year he had won the national doubles title with Tilden, and he was playing a game that I had no conceivable right to be on any closer terms with than that of spectator, turning my head one way and then the other to watch the ball in play. But here I was engaging it across a net, and the sensation was that of keeping company with a bird, high in the sky, and looking down on all the earthbound creatures far below. Playing with somebody a lot better than you are serves to elevate your own game unrecognizably above its customary level.

Playing with Harry Shub did much the same, compared to the way I would have floundered in the thickets of that Vivaldi if, one day at home, I had picked that music up and tried to make my way through it alone.

The same thing applied, in turn, to the Mozart concertos, the Strassburg Number Four, Turkish Number Five, and Scottish or Edinburgh Number Three. I got through them. Not with grace or any sort of finesse, not with sparkle or élan or any semblance of aplomb, but British army style, muddling through and losing every battle except the last one.

But not even the redoubtable Mr. Shub could carry me through those Joachim cadenzas. We had to leave them, reluctantly but inevitably, until "the next time around for this concerto, after you've licked a few other things." The same was true of the cadenzas to the Fifth Concerto. It wasn't until we came to the easier but still beautiful San Franko cadenzas for the Third, which seem so much more inherently and integrally Mozartian than Joachim's Hungarian floridities, that I was able to negotiate a Mozart concerto without skipping the cadenzas.

It was along in here, and as we were going through the three Brahms sonatas, that Mr. Shub began practicing the calculated cruelty of seeing to it that I was at all times bogged down with some one bête noire, in the form of a set task exacted as the price of letting me play a new Kreisler number and a new Mozart sonata. These were rationed out to me, like dessert as a reward for eating my spinach, and I had some eighteen of each doled out to me while I was gagging and chewing on some half-dozen of the items in the "hard work" category that I soon came to regard as just so much spinach, and so would have been inclined to say the hell with.

The first of these was the Saint-Saëns *Introduction and Rondo Capriccioso*, with its middle passage in double stops, which should be so dreamily beautiful, and its last two passages of *spiccato* bowing, which should be so light and sparkling. In both instances these still came out for me like lumps in the mashed potatoes that no amount of beating and whipping is sufficient to eradicate.

The next was the first of the Bach sonatas and partitas for violin alone, where my poor fiddle, called upon to make like an organ with those multitudinous four-string chords, squeaks like rusty springs instead, especially in the *Fugue*. The *Adagio* and *Sicilienne* I can play nearly from memory, but I still flounder like a netted fish when I get enmeshed in the *Fugue*. The last movement is undoubtedly the easiest of the four, except that I so seldom reach it, after bogging down for so long in the *Fugue* that there's barely enough fiddling time left in almost any practice session to get beyond the *Sicilienne*.

Fiddling practice sessions that include such things as these, and such other black beasts as the Vitali *Ciaccona*, Corelli's *La Folia*, almost any part of the Mendelssohn Concerto in E Minor, and even such a pesky little nuisance as Hubay's *Hejre Kati*, cannot humanely be conducted, or committed—to use a more fitting term—where Janie is likely to be submitted to the cruel and unusual punishment of hearing me practice them. So, for such items, I confine my fiddling to the earliest hours of the day. During the week, at the office, it can be heard only by Manny Hoffman, who gets in at four-thirty, two hours ahead of me every day, and is long since inured to even the most exotic of sounds. On Saturdays and Sundays I take quite literally to the tall timbers at the break of day, going up to the log cabin at the Joe Jefferson Club, where I can be heard by nobody at all. This is a fishing club I belong to, in Saddle River five minutes away from my house, and the clubhouse sits in the middle of a wooded tract, at the end of a long driveway, where at five in the morning there is nobody within earshot for several hundred yards in every direction. There the early morning world is safe even for Bach fugues on the violin alone.

This last is directed not against Bach, but rather against myself. I love both the first two Bach violin concertos, which never made my bête noire list. Further, the Bach Concerto for Two Violins has been a great favorite of mine since the days when I used to play it for myself, in the Kreisler-Zimbalist rendition, whenever there were no customers at Friedrich's Music Store in Grand Rapids. This was after school, when, as a high-school kid, I served as the Red Seal specialist in the record department there. My affection for that concerto has even survived what I used to do to it back in 1936 when Linda Denby and I would play it on her two Klozes, before one of them was mine, in the oval music room of our house on North State Parkway in Chicago.

But even eighteen Mozart sonatas and an approximately equal amount of vintage Kreisler cannot entirely assuage the agonies that are still contained for me in that one Bach fugue, and I doubt that life can be long enough to enable me to look back on it, from some unlikely future peak of proficiency, with tolerant amusement at its diminished size from that distant perspective, as a petty obstacle long since overcome.

Some of these black beasts may yet be tamed. The horrors of the *Rondo Capriccioso* are no longer as savage as they once seemed, and there are moments now when *La Folia* seems almost benign, at least when I recall its first palpable malignancy of a couple of years back.

But I can still look just as incredulous as ever, whenever Harry Shub now says, as he so often does, "This may come as a shock to you, but I think we're going to make a pretty fair fiddler of you yet."

TEN

had got through over a year without buying more than a shoulder pad or a string or a cake of rosin, and probably would have been about ready to begin manifesting some withdrawal symptoms, when something happened that served to reinforce and prolong the transference of my fiddle mania from collecting to playing.

I got a call from Joe Eger, the horn player since turned conductor, asking me, of all things, if I had ever thought of playing my fiddle in public.

I answered that I had been known to entertain some crazy thoughts in my time, but that such an extreme aberration as that had never occurred to me. I added that if he ever heard one of my tapes he'd understand why.

I had served with Joe Eger on a discussion panel that met weekly in the fall of 1967 at the New School for Social Research, and had seen him again in Pittsburgh that following spring, at the sessions of the annual convention of the American Symphony Orchestra League. Later that summer, when I was holed up in the New York Public Library for my annual estivation on a writing project, he called my office to see if I could have breakfast with him any day soon, and early enough so that I could still get down to the library on time for its nine o'clock opening. He said he wanted to pick my brains.

Since the work I was doing at the library was on a book about business and the arts, I welcomed the idea of a brain-picking session with Joe Eger, who had struck me as a most knowledgeable man about the arts. But it was with the proverbial one thought for him and two for me that I agreed to meet him, as I figured his would be the brain that would get the more avidly picked. I was particularly interested in a mixed-media concert he had conducted that spring at the Garden State Arts Center, in which he had featured rock groups along with the members of the American Symphony Orchestra, which he had served for the two previous seasons as Stokowski's associate conductor.

It developed, when I met him for breakfast at his place up in the neighborhood of Harry Shub's studio near Lincoln Center, that he was exploring the possibilities of doing more things in this direction, of trying to make the symphony more relevant to the interests of today's younger audiences. He was in fact engaged in forming a new symphonic group, dedicated to the Mahomet-like principle that if the people wouldn't come to the symphony some means should be sought of bringing the symphony to the people.

I applauded the concept, for which he had revived the old New York Orchestral Society, dormant for some years, since it seemed to me that he was at least fumbling for one of the right keys to the closing of the audience gap that has plagued serious music, along with the rest of the performed arts, across the country. I suggested, since he wanted my advice on forming a board and seeking business and foundation support, that he try to get some prominent business figure known for his friendship for the arts, who would have both the time to devote to such a project and the influence essential to its success—somebody like Devereux Josephs, the retired chairman of the New York Life Insurance Company, who had been a member of the Rockefeller Panel on the Performing Arts and was well known as a friend of arts groups. If they lacked a leader of that stature, I doubted that a place could be carved out for a new symphonic group in such a musically overendowed center as New York. I agreed to serve as a spear carrier on his board, whenever formed, always subject to the circumstance that its key figure might or might not want to avail himself of my services.

Joe wanted to know if he could "use my name" and I said sure, why not, and since I had no further suggestions to offer and it was getting on for nine, I left.

After that I saw Joe much more frequently than I had before, usually at meetings for which we let him use our exhibit hall in the office, during the formative stages of his new orchestra, The Symphony of New York.

Somewhat to my surprise, the new orchestra's first mixed-media affair turned out to be held not, as I would have expected, at some place in the garment center, or some settlement on the Lower East Side, or up in Harlem or over in Brooklyn, but at Carnegie Hall. And, not in the least to my surprise, it turned out to be an artistic success and a financial disaster. The reviews and the publicity across the country were excellent, and the precipitation of red ink was as great, for one concert, as most struggling young arts groups are prepared to expect for an entire season.

It was with the hope of doing something about the orchestra's financial difficulties, after the Carnegie Hall concert and before the next one, scheduled for Philharmonic Hall in the early spring, that Joe had called me up to ask if I'd ever thought of playing my fiddle in public. As I say, I had warned him that hearing one of my tapes would probably end any thought that he might have entertained on the subject.

But Joe Eger is as brave as he is resourceful, and he's always getting people to do unlikely things for good enough reason, which he somehow manages to muster, so I wasn't too surprised when he came around, right after that, to hear one of my tapes.

It was one I had just played for Harry Shub the day before, and happened still to have in the machine at my office. By the weekend it would have been erased, as it merely represented my current point of progress in the two newest things I was working on, the Nardini Concerto in E Minor and Mozart's first concerto, the Adelaide, written in 1766 at the age of ten for the Dauphine of France.

Joe, listening to them both with his eye on his wristwatch, opted for the Nardini on the basis that it ran, without the repeats—the way I always play everything to save both Mr. Shub's time and my tape—only eleven minutes, as opposed to almost seventeen for the Adelaide.

"It'll sound a lot better," Joe said, "with a good pianist doing the accompaniment, and we'll get you a good one."

"But where? You don't really mean in public, do you?"

"Well, not exactly, but it'll be either a small hall or a large home."

And that was all I could get out of him for weeks thereafter. He said it would probably be the last week in January, because he knew I wouldn't be getting back from a cruise until the middle of that month, and that it would have to be no later than mid-February or it would be too late to do any good for the Philharmonic Hall concert. What he had in mind was a fund-raising party, at which various well-intentioned amateurs, of whom I was to be one, would perform.

A small hall or a large home—and a good pianist—that was all I was to know, and indeed all I had to know, though I was naturally curious as to who and how many his other trained seals might be.

But I set to work on the Nardini as though, if not my life, then at least a conservatory Grand Prix depended on it. I began memorizing it, both with and without the fiddle in hand, visualizing the notes as I played them either in actuality or on the tape recorder, with the earphones, on buses and subways and in waiting rooms—indeed, wherever I found myself with even a few minutes to devote to it, as if more than my fortune and my sacred honor depended on it.

I soon had it down, I thought, cold. All three movements, and if need arose, the repeats of the first half of each of them. That was true even before I went on the cruise, and there, at every opportunity, day or night, I played it through over and over again, by day with the heavy practice mute, and at night silently, going through all the motions with both hands, but with the bow held so far over at an angle as to escape any actual hair contact with the strings.

What Mr. Shub had wanted to know right away, when I first told him about the recital, was what I was going to do for an encore. I had never thought of that.

"Give 'em two," he suggested. "They'll have to call you back for one as a matter of course, common courtesy demands it, and if you give them two, one right after the other, you'll be sparing them any need to decide whether they ought to call you back more than once. That'll settle it. Besides, there's always the safety factor that if you mess up one you'll probably do all right on the other."

So, again on the safety-first principle, we picked the two Kreisler tunes I knew best, to be bracketed as my encore: *Rondino*, of which I'd always had a phonograph record since 1917, and *Liebesleid*. The latter, while much less showy than its accustomed companion piece, *Liebesfreud*, is a much safer bet because it's slower, and, with its two main sections simply repeated, is much easier to remember. Besides, I'd known it, like *Rondino*, literally forever, while I had only recently negotiated *Liebesfreud* for the first time in studying it with Mr. Shub, along with a dozen other Kreisler numbers that I had never played before. The two encore numbers also got the same day and night treatment, either muted or silent, that I gave the Nardini throughout the cruise.

When I got back to town it was to find that the time and place for the party had at last been set, and that it was to be just a month away, on February 16, at the new Park Avenue apartment of Mr. and Mrs. Bernard J. Relin, whom it could serve as a housewarming as well as a party for the orchestra's benefit.

Also, I knew now who my accompanist was going to be. He was Edwin Hymowitz, whom I had heard of as an accompanist to real fiddlers, and there was a number where I could reach him and arrange a few rehearsals before the actual event.

The only trouble with that was that for days on end the phone never answered, and I was about to give up and ask Joe for another pianist when at last on a Saturday morning I reached him. The reason I had not been able to get him before, though I had called all day and evening for three days, was simple enough. He and his wife were reverse commuters, teaching in an upstate college through the week and coming back to their apartment at Seventy-fourth and Lexington on Saturdays and Sundays, when they both had some pupils and she sang on Sunday morning in the church around the corner on Madison Avenue.

Thinking there was no reason she should have to suffer, just because my own wife was the involuntary listener to my fiddling, I arranged to come for rehearsal on Sunday morning during the time Mrs. Hymowitz was at church, singing for the service. I hoped to repeat the procedure on each of the four remaining Sundays before the date of the event for which we were preparing.

On the first Sunday, I was momentarily thrown by the realization that there were gaps in the music, where the piano is heard and the violin is silent—something I had just never bothered to notice before, since I had learned these things, and practiced them, without accompaniment of any sort, not even, as I now regretted, the stamp of my own foot. Furthermore, aside from these prolonged rests, there were a number of places, particularly bothersome in the Nardini, where the violin is obliged to sustain notes longer than I had ever seen any sense in doing just for my own edification, on which sustained notes the piano hangs little filigrees of ornamentation. Very pretty, except that I hadn't realized they were there and hence didn't wait for them to happen.

Hymowitz is a natural diplomat. He suggested that perhaps my playing of the Nardini could use "a little less *rubato*."

There couldn't have been found a more flattering way of conveying the homely truth that the way I was playing the Nardini, as far as the rhythmical give and take with the piano was concerned, was chaotic.

But Hymowitz was so good that the trouble was straightened out very quickly, and once we got into the swing of doing the three numbers a few times together, I soon began to realize that a good accompanist is as unobtrusively efficient about keeping out of your way as a good dancer is. I've danced with women who were so good that I couldn't have stepped on their feet if I'd tried, and Hymowitz was as good as that with his fingers.

If I fell, he would dip right with me, and make it look as if we'd planned to do it that way. Let me skip four bars and I would find that he had skipped them too, and we were as together as the hands of the clock at five after one.

Before the morning was over we had the Nardini in the can, so to speak, reduced to a pretty good representation on tape, and the following Sunday the same could be said of the two Kreisler encores. The Sunday after that the Kreisler numbers went even better, perhaps because, in addition to being Groundhog Day, it was also Kreisler's ninety-fourth birthday.

But the Sunday after that was the day of the big storm that left the city hog-tied for a week, and that day we missed our practice, not because I couldn't get in, for I did, and only ten minutes later than I had arrived the two Sundays before, but because we couldn't find the music.

It had been on the piano, Ed said, the day before, when a student had been there for a lesson. He assumed that his wife had "tidied up" since then, but that it must be somewhere. The apartment is small and we had ransacked it, looking for those three missing piano parts, within ten minutes. Then we called his wife, at the church around the corner, where he knew she wasn't actually due to "go on" in the service for another fifteen minutes. But she hadn't touched the music, hated being disturbed at church, and suggested that it was much more likely that the mother of yesterday's pupil, in gathering up her music, had taken it along by mistake. So he called her. She hated being called on a Sunday morning, hated still more to be "accused of taking somebody else's property."

By this time I began to think I had caused enough trouble for one morning, and, besides, I could see out the window that the storm was looking much worse by the minute. Although I had come in without any real difficulty beyond that of keeping the windshield reasonably clear, I had been annoyed by the cheery insistence with which successive announcers kept reading predictions of a snowfall of from two to four inches when one look outside would have told them that it was already from six to eight inches deep.

So I took off, after arranging to make up for this missed day of rehearsal by having an extra one, a sort of dress rehearsal, the morning of the 16th, the day of the actual performance.

It was a good thing we didn't find the music (it later developed that the kid's mother had scooped it up after the lesson), because a couple of hours later I wouldn't have made it back home. As it was, I made it by dint of maneuvering around stalled cars until I got to my own driveway, where I stalled halfway to the garage.

During these weeks of preparation, Harry Shub, at my Wednesday lessons, seemed much more perturbed about the Nardini than

I was. He kept pointing out places where it would be easy to take the wrong turning, so to speak, and go back rather than forward, in each of the three movements. He also wondered that I wasn't nervous about it, and seemed to regard this as almost a bad sign.

I said I supposed it was simply because I was so used to speaking in public that I probably regarded this as just another appearance like any other, and might well discover to my great embarrassment and chagrin that it wasn't.

He assured me that it wasn't the same thing at all, and kept telling me scary tales about this and that famous performer who, even after fifty years of playing in public since child-prodigy days, still had to be literally propelled out on stage, because each time they were so convinced that this was one time they just simply, literally, physically, couldn't go on.

But they still went on, and probably nobody but those in the wings who pushed them ever knew they had a care in the world, I assumed.

Yes, usually, but then he would recall instances of hideous memory lapses in public performances, wherein this or that well-known fiddler was obliged to stop, walk over, and look at the accompanist's score, and in one or two instances even remain there, using the notes to the end of the number.

I sensed that this last, if not apocryphal, was probably not as frequent an occurrence as he implied, and wondered if he wasn't perhaps just telling me things like that to make me feel better if in dire emergency I were to find myself obliged to do the same thing.

But he insisted that these were not made-up stories, and that he remembered one time when, of all things, it had happened with *Rondino*, this very Kreisler number I was playing, and of all people, to Mischa Elman, to whom the piece was dedicated. Elman had decided to give it as an encore, the first, after a particularly taxing program he had just concluded at Carnegie Hall. Shub thought perhaps he did it because he knew Kreisler was there, or, if not actually there, because he knew he was in town and would hear about it.

One portion of *Rondino* has some downward slides, before and after some upward ones, that are very similar, and it's extremely easy to get stuck on doing them the way they occur the first time, without applying the relatively slight change that occurs in them the second time around.

This Elman forgot to do, not only when he came to them the first time, but twice more, when he reached them again after filling in with the upward slides that are like the slice of meat between the two sides of a sandwich. It was the third time that, rather than stay on in perpetual motion, where his accompanist was loyally following him, he walked over to the piano and hitched a ride on its score.

Never having known either Kreisler or Elman I wondered why all the stories I've ever heard about Elman seem to put him down, whereas all the Kreisler stories tend to build Kreisler up. Shub had no clue, beyond feeling that Kreisler was twice the man that Elman was, meaning by that, I suppose, that Kreisler was so many more things, quite apart from fiddling proficiency, than Elman could have hoped to be, such as composer, pianist, and great authority, as well as collector, on such recondite bookish matters as incunabula.

So I told Shub the old Kreisler story, but new to me as it seemed to be to him, that I had from John McFadyen, who had told it at the Manhattan College of Music, about the time Kreisler was lunching at the Ritz in Boston and two very prim and proper Boston ladies stopped at his table and asked him to autograph their menu for them, saying they couldn't restrain the impulse to tell him how much happiness he had given them, over how many years.

FRITZ KREISLER, *aetat.* 81, WITH A BOOK

Simone Fernando Sacconi

"Yes," one said, "my sister and I were just saying, it goes away back to 1924, when they first came out, and do you know, we've never since driven anything but one of your cars!"

So Kreisler duly autographed the menu, taking great care with the spelling, and conveying the appreciation and best wishes of Walter P. Chrysler.

Mr. Shub couldn't think of a topper for that one, so he asked me instead whether I'd ever heard Harriet Kreisler's great line, "Think what a violinist Fritz could have been if only he'd practiced."

My own practice, lacking the kind of talent that makes practice superfluous, went doggedly on until the day of the concert, when the dress rehearsal in the morning, which we put on tape, convinced me that I had all three numbers down cold and could forget about them until the actual moment of playing them.

The party began with drinks, of course, and, remembering

that every time I'd had lunch with Rafael on the day of a night when he had to play in a concert he would never touch a drop of anything more than tomato juice, I was prudent enough to ask for plain tonic water on the rocks.

I had long ago, when I was getting over an allergic reaction to a wrong antibiotic, discovered that this is the best of non-drinks for a drinking occasion. People never notice it, assuming it's either gin or vodka. But Shub noticed it, and turned apoplectic at the sight. Even when I reassured him, saying that I didn't intend to have a drink of any other sort until after I had played, it still seemed to me that he was acting as fidgety as a clucking mother hen.

"Did you check the Strad since you got here? Is it all right? Is it in a safe place? Where you going to warm up?"

Huh? Warming up is something I thought baseball pitchers did, in a place called a bullpen. How was I to know that fiddlers never go on in public until they have warmed up? I pointed out that I had had a dress rehearsal in the morning, and that everything had gone off letter perfect, and I thought the best thing was not to think about it again until I actually got up to play.

This seemed to upset him more than the sight of what he had thought was a drink.

"Good rehearsal's a bad sign," he said. "I'd sooner things had been lousy this morning, so I'd know those bloopers were out of your system. You've got a bad habit, you know, of making the worst ones on the easiest parts, or whenever you come to the parts you think you know best."

I said yes, I knew that, and reminded him again of my likeness to the near-illiterate who misspells only the easy words because the hard ones he has to look up.

"Yes, that's a very good analogy," he said, as if I'd never mentioned it before, and looked more agitated than ever.

Who the hell's playing this concert, I wondered, is he or am I? He seemed to be having shakes enough for both of us. Like the deadbeat discussing a bill he has no intention of paying, I felt there was no reason we should both be worried about it. But to make him feel better I said I'd get the Strad from under the piano where I'd put it when I first came in, and find Mr. Relin and see if I could have a place to warm up, just before time to go on, meanwhile leaving the Strad in whatever room was to be designated my bullpen.

But since the performance wasn't to be until after dinner, the main salon where the recital was to be held was barred across its door with white satin ribbon, like the pews at a church wedding. This had been done since my arrival, and I had a time getting under the barriers and coming out again, with the Strad in its cumbersome Lady Tennant princess-coffin case, on my hands and knees.

I think it must have been for some adolescent, show-off reason that I brought it in that satinwood coffer and put it under the new and splendid Bechstein concert grand with the thought of taking it out of its gorgeous setting, nonchalantly, to bedazzle the assembled multitude—an aim (if I had it and I must have, else why not bring it in from Jersey in its nine-ounce Jaeger traveling case?) in which I was now neatly foiled by Shub's insistence that I take it to the place where I was to warm up.

This turned out to be Mr. Relin's bedroom, and the minute we were in there Mr. Shub insisted on getting the Strad and the Dodd bow out and satisfying himself that they were both in shape to pass his most rigorous inspection, though what he could have done about it if they weren't I couldn't imagine, as it hadn't occurred to either of us to have a spare fiddle there for untoward contingencies.

He played the Strad, to make sure it was in perfect tune, choosing a double-stop passage from the Brahms concerto, on which he made it sound like an organ in a cathedral. He never trusted me, even in the privacy of his studio, to get my own fiddle properly in tune, but always did it for me, and now, on a great occasion like my debut, he was still less inclined to let me monkey with it for that purpose.

As he played, I figured that the hundred and more people gathered in the foyer for drinks could hear every note, and I toyed with the idea, if he played long enough, of coming up with some picturesque indisposition when the time came for me to play, so I could quit winner, so to speak, sure that everybody there would go home convinced that I could have given a terrific performance based on the sample they must surely have heard.

But he stopped, as suddenly as he had begun, and after trying the four strings again to satisfy himself that it couldn't be tuned any finer, began giving me precise and elaborate instructions on how to *pretend* to be tuning it myself, when I first got out in front of the audience.

"That first impression is terribly important," he said. "You must give them time to get settled, and the way you deliberate over your tuning helps to reassure them that everything is all right, and you know your business. You must act very hard to be pleased with the tuning, and keep pretending to make adjustments so minute they won't hear them. Any pros there may be in the audience will know what you're doing and why you're doing it—because they would do the same thing, so you don't have to worry about them; they'll only be surprised if you get through the program without breaking down [the first time this horrid thought had even occurred to me]—and the rest will all be impressed with what a terrific ear you have. Don't worry, I'll have your fiddle in perfect tune before I let you take it out there, after you've warmed up."

By now he was beginning to make me nervous too, which I hadn't had sense enough to be, up to that point. But, my God, what if I *did* break down? The dress rehearsal that morning, and the previous Sundays with Hymowitz, had completely reassured me on that score. But what if I did?

"Oh don't worry—just holler 'Harry!'—none of that Mr. Shub business—and I'll come running and get you back on the track."

A less likely recourse than that I couldn't have thought up in a week's trying. We had never called each other anything but Mister in over two years, and I even thought it was pretty good that I called him just plain Mister and not Maestro, although he is twenty years my junior, or thereabouts.

"Oh, and after the tuning, don't forget to examine the bow very critically—pretend to give the nut a very slight twist, and look at the head plate as if you thought it might have come loose. You know it hasn't, but it also helps the audience to settle down and it gives them more reassurance. And don't forget that Hymowitz will be looking at you all this time, but you don't look at him. You only turn to give him the nod after you've taken your own sweet time with all this business of the tuning and the bow."

"What nod? He's got eight bars before I come in on the Nardini, and he knows I can catch him if he starts before I give him any nod."

"But he wouldn't dream of it. Don't forget that, unlike you, he's a pro. He'd be committing professional suicide. A good accompanist will sit there all evening, just looking at you and never batting an eye, just waiting for the signal to begin."

Sounded like the Prussian army to me, but I promised I wouldn't forget to nod. So we left, to rejoin the others who were having drinks, and without Mr. Shub's asking me to play at all. I took it that his own playing had somewhat eased his tension, and that he was content, now that I had agreed not to go on without first warming up.

It would have been ladies first, if the original program had been followed, as a girl who was a professional actress but not a professional singer was the only other performer Joe Eger had been able to line up for his amateur night fund-raising party, and at next to the last minute, actually the day before the event, she had come down with the Hong Kong flu and been obliged to cancel. Under the circumstances, all he could do was call on some of his first-chair players from the orchestra to fill out the evening. Not, thank God, his concertmaster, Sanford Allen, a superb Negro violinist, and the only one I ever knew except Eddie South, who used to be billed in the old days as "The Dark Angel of the Violin." That would have been as bad as having Harry Shub play on the same program. Actually, Allen was there, and was in fact the only person to come into my "green room" to see the Strad. He was green with envy of it, having not long before lost out on getting the Lord Norton Strad of 1737, which contends with the famous Chant du Cygne of the same year for the distinction of being the last instrument to leave the master's hands. At the time it was still available he couldn't swing the financing of its purchase for his use, and by the time he could it was gone. (He has since acquired the Kneisel Strad of 1714, which I happen to consider a much greater fiddle).

But there was another string man on the program at that, to my dismay. Joe said he would explain that away to the audience, convincing them that the cello was a much less exacting instrument to play than the violin, but all I could think of was that Kreisler always said that Casals was the greatest string player the world had ever known, and the thought of going on as even the most well-meaning of amateurs after a professional on another bowed string instrument was more than I could face. The cellist was going to play a Bach suite for cello alone, and, knowing what a mess I would have made of my one Bach sonata for unaccompanied violin, I felt that this news confirmed my worst fears. The other numbers were to be done by a clarinetist and an oboist, so I had no cause to worry directly about them, but Joe did see my point about putting me on before any other player, since the others were all professionals.

Naturally, I thought that dinner would never end, as I was anxious to do my stint and get it over with, and while I hadn't been nervous at all when I first arrived, Shub's constant fluttering around to take my psychic temperature was beginning to get to me, and I felt for the first time some semblance of qualms over having agreed to play in this almost-public ambiance that combined both Joe's promises of a small hall in a large home. I found it harder and harder to wait until the now around one hundred twenty-five diners had finished their dessert and I could get to the warm-up place and feel the satisfying sensation, through the

Gudgeon's strings, that the Nardini was still there where I had left it so comfortably ensconced that morning. I didn't wonder at all about the two Kreisler numbers, as I knew that if I didn't get through the three movements of the Nardini I'd have no need for them anyway. Besides, I figured I could play them standing on my head in a dark closet, whereas Shub had worried me over how easy it was to take the wrong turning, after the repeat of the first half, in each of the Concerto's three movements.

I thought that, whenever I at last got to Mr. Relin's bedroom for the warm-up during the time it would take for all the diners to get from the dining room and the corridors and the library where little café dining tables had been set up, and settled in the large room that was going to serve as the promised "small hall," I would just play through the danger spots that I knew Mr. Shub meant, in each of the Nardini movements after the repeat, to make certainty doubly sure that I did, in each case, know the right turning to take. I felt sure of the last two movements in this respect, but now suddenly found myself entertaining a small doubt about that juncture in the first movement, despite the fact that in all the rehearsals with Ed Hymowitz it had always gone without a hitch.

But when I finally got to my "green room" I found it wasn't mine any more. It had been completely empty when Mr. Relin had led me there with Shub, and indeed the Strad was still there in its gleaming satinwood case, where I had left it on the bed, but so was a huge cello case, next to it by the bed, and so was a huge cellist, a young fellow seated on a boudoir chair that he had taken from the dressing table, and so absorbed in tearing off the double stops of the Bach suite, to the obvious delectation of his girl friend on the chaise longue next to the dressing table, that neither of them seemed to see or hear me when I came in.

So, not knowing what else to do, and knowing that the warm-up time was too short to be wasted in any excursions looking for Mr. Relin through the crowds getting up from little tables all along the corridor, I picked up Strad and Dodd and went into the bathroom and shut the door.

When I essayed the first of the Nardini danger spots, the cello brayed right on, not dropping so much as one note of a succession of Bach triple and even quadruple chords, so I kept on, too. I figured it didn't matter so much whether I could hear myself as that I should satisfy myself that my fingers knew the feel of all three of the right turnings, and assumed that I wouldn't be bothering the cellist, as obviously orchestra players must be used to sawing and tootling away right next to each other at every practice opportunity. I was relieved to find that my fingers seemed to know the way perfectly past the tricky points where it is easy to be thrown back into the first half of each of the three movements, once past the repeat in each case.

When I got to the "wings," in the now deserted dining room, on one side of an arch through which I could see into the salon where the audience was now all assembled, I checked, while waiting for Joe Eger to begin his introduction, to see that the pianist's wife, Natacha Hymowitz, was installed with my tape recorder on the floor in front of the first row of chairs, where she had agreed to be.

I wanted this performance on tape, if only to prove to myself later that I hadn't dreamed this whole affair, and had taken the precaution of making sure, the minute I arrived, that somebody would be detailed to see to it that every minute of the actual performance was taken down on tape. My part of the program, even including all the repeats on the Nardini and the two hoped-for Kreisler encores, would be about twenty-two minutes of playing time, and I had provided the recorder with new batteries and a fresh tape, to make certain that nothing went wrong. Mrs. Hymowitz had explained that she knew nothing about tape recorders, and I had said, "Good, that way I won't worry. As long as you don't pick it up or touch it, but just move this one button this way when you want it to record, and that way when you want it to stop, nothing can go wrong."

She was there all right, as I could see by peeking around the corner of the arch, from the darkened dining room, but so were quite a few other people, seated companionably beside her on the floor, apparently having been moved to follow her example and get in the very first row, rather than take some seats they could have had at the far end of the room, back by the other arch, behind which Janie sat alone in her chair in the library. She had been queening it there, all through cocktail and dinnertime, as people who hadn't seen her since before she was sick some five years before came to see her, and I was perfectly content to have her stay there, at least through my part of the performance, out of sight if not of hearing.

After I had gone through all the precautions of checking the taping, I relaxed and sat back to enjoy Joe's introduction. Joe Eger is a natural as a speaker, and I knew he would do a good job, both of acquainting the audience with the aims and achievements of The Symphony of New York as well as putting them in exactly the right frame of mind to sympathize with the aims, if not the achievements, of his amateur performer, a heretofore blameless collector who was tonight manifesting his first aspiration to become known, if only for this once, as the rich man's Jack Benny.

Joe did such a good job of making them understand how hideously difficult the violin is to play that, as he warmed to his theme of making it sound like a small miracle that this hand up here and that hand waving out there should ever contrive to coordinate in such a way as to produce an acceptable noise, I began to think of his whole presentation in terms of a stock-offering brochure in which, to meet SEC requirements, such dire possibilities must be spelled out as to make the reader feel that he would be a certifiable idiot to buy any of the shares so described. I was fully prepared to have everybody agree that the thing he pantomimed was so fantastically and outrageously hard to do that it would be only sensible to let it go at that, as palpably impossible, and pass on to the next act.

But a moment was soon to arrive when I wished that he had made the case a little stronger.

I was fine on the fake tuning and the fussy fondling of the faultless bow, and I duly gave the nod, not so much as a second too soon, to Ed Hymowitz, after I had milked the silence, per Shub's instructions, to that point known as a deadly hush, and I even gave an extra nod to his wife, something the script hadn't called for, to indicate that it was time to push that little button.

The sound of Hymowitz in the opening measures of the Nardini on that beautiful Bechstein was so normal, so coolly competent and assured, that any thought I might have had of stage fright vanished at once. This was just doing of a Sunday evening what we had been doing of a Sunday morning for weeks, and as he reached the point of my entry I sailed in with aplomb.

I was startled by my first note to discover that the Gudgeon, which I'd always thought of as being a violin for small rooms, now sounded big as all outdoors, but I rather relished the thought that for once I didn't have to keep it down but could intone it for all it was worth.

On the second phrase, my forefinger somehow nicked the corner of the Strad's upper bout, and the bow bounced so springily, from that slightest of contacts, that I was afraid it was going to fly right out of my grasp and into the room.

Hmm, so this was a sample of what they'd always warned me about—the crazy unexpected things that would inevitably happen to you in performance but would never happen in the privacy of a practice session.

But the Dodd, except for that brief vagary of jumping as suddenly as a goosed dowager, behaved immediately thereafter as beautifully as it always had from the first day I'd played it, and I relaxed, rather pleased that this unexpected break had not thrown me off to the extent of missing a note.

I ventured a look around the room, and was surprised to see that, although the fiddle sounded loud to me as a fire siren, everyone looked as composed and still as if they were about to doze off. I didn't know what I could do about that, so I decided it would be

better not to look around, and concentrated instead on a particular pane of glass in one of the tall curtained windows.

Everything was going fine, and I was just beginning to enjoy myself when, as I was rounding the turn of the first half of the first movement, for the repeat, I heard a tapping noise almost at my feet and turned to see, in horror, that some big oaf sitting next to Natacha Hymowitz on the floor, in the row before the first row of those who were seated, had picked up the tape recorder from where she had placed it before her on the carpet,

and was tapping it, blowing on it, and generally treating it in the manner of a zoo monkey examining a strange object thrown into his cage.

Oh God, no, no, no, I started to shake my head, and was startled to realize that in doing so I was causing the Strad to emit some short, sharp, and very monkeylike squeaks.

I wanted to stop and say, "The hell with the Nardini, what do you think you're doing to my tape recorder?" but figured that by now the damage was probably done, and went right on play-ing, confining myself to an imploring look at Mrs. Hymowitz as I did so.

She gave the conventional little shoulder shrug of helpless dis-tress and I decided I'd better not risk looking at either of them any more, or I'd surely muff the next turn in the first move-ment of the concerto. I was very much surprised that I hadn't faltered or slowed down or done anything out of kilter after that first involuntary gasp that my headshake had elicited from the fiddle.

Ed was playing right on as if nothing had happened, reminding me—here I had a fleeting impulse to giggle, which I managed to stifle—of how as a kid I had, for the pleasure of my playmates in a lumber yard, impersonated a member of the ship's orchestra on the *Titanic*, fiddling away with two sticks on *Nearer My God to Thee* as the ship went down. But to my amazement, after the big upset over the taping incident, I was still playing on just as calmly as the imperturbable Hymowitz.

I judged that we had probably covered the first minute and a half of the fifteen minutes that the three movements of the Nardini take with all the repeats, and I felt pretty sure that it represented all I would have as a souvenir on tape of my per-formance. Like a fragment of a piece of pottery dug up by an archeologist, the rest would have to be guessed at from that.

I was very conscious of having passed what I was sure were the worst of the two danger spots, after the repeated passage in the first two movements, and realized that I had literally seen on the wall, as if projected on a movie screen, the measures contain-ing the key notes that differentiated the second turnings from the first, in both instances. Since I hadn't ever really worried about either of the other two bad spots, after successfully negotiating the crucial turn in the first movement, I now began to feel a sort of "home stretch" burst of confidence. The horse was headed for the barn.

The last movement of the Nardini is technically the hardest, by a considerable margin, because it has two passages of double stops, interspersed with rapidly accelerating chords across all four strings, making for the only really showy portions of the entire concerto, which is, for the most part, serenely melodic and graceful. But as part of my peculiar semiliterate pattern of getting the hard parts right and having trouble only with the easy ones, I had always romped right through this movement without any faltering at all, even before I had begun to memorize the work as a whole and was still having fairly hard going with the first two movements.

So now, as I rounded the turn after the repeat of the movement's first half, where the rest of the way was—with about a minute and a half to go—strictly "all downhill to the finish line," suddenly a whistle blew inside my head, as insistently as a traffic cop's signal to stop.

I froze, or at least I thought I did.

What concerto? All I knew was that suddenly I didn't know another note.

This was the moment, I dimly realized, when I was supposed to yell, "Harry!" But that was unthinkable. What was thinkable? I wondered. Isn't there some procedure for a case like this—some little red wagon that runs out onto the field to remove you? Or men in white with a stretcher?

I didn't know what to do, since I was trying to do something I had never done before, and to the best of my knowledge and recollection I did nothing. Somewhere, far off, I could hear a piano and, very odd, a violin. But where the sound was coming from I couldn't imagine.

I suppose this wasn't the same form of stage fright that is the dread of a singer, where a hand suddenly seems to grab the throat and choke off all sound, as was reported to have happened to poor Ganna Walska at the Chicago Opera more often than not.

But it must have been something very similar to what happens to a boxer when he's "up Queer Street," for I was certainly out on my feet. I didn't know where I was or who I was or what I was doing or even what I was supposed to be doing. I would testify under oath that I knew absolutely nothing of what happened after I passed that point in the last movement that marks the end of the repeat. I couldn't say "everything went all white," but if I had to vote for one I'd probably pick black, because white is the sum of color and black is its absence, and thus seems better to me to mark the void that represented the spot where I stood. I just wasn't there. I don't know where I was, because I wasn't anywhere that I remember anything about.

That I was sound asleep with my eyes open—or if not asleep, in any case dead to the world—must have been the situation during that last minute and a half of the performance, because I remember coming to with a start—whether "awake" or "alive" I can't honestly distinguish—at the sharp burst of the sound of applause.

My muscles were so used to the pattern of that last movement that they simply finished the job for me, like a bunch of non-coms going calmly on to the end of the action after the last field officer falls.

After a suitable interval, Hymowitz and I came out again, and polished off the two Kreisler numbers without incident. Nor was anybody very ready to believe me when I said that I had finished the Nardini while I was literally out on my feet. I think they thought I was fishing for compliments.

All I knew for sure was that if anybody had noticed anything it would be Janie. But she had been seated, around the corner from the arch leading into the far end of the room, where she was out of sight if not of sound. All I could get out of her, when I rejoined her there after putting the Strad away, was,

"Well, you were dreadful, but I must say I have heard you play that Nardini better than you played it here tonight."

This made me wish, more than ever, that I had a tape of the whole performance, to see if I could detect any difference in the sound of that portion which, when I heard it at all, while going under my momentary anaesthetic, so to speak, sounded so very far away, in contrast to how loud the Strad had seemed in my ears when I first started to play.

But my worst fears had been realized. The tape ran just for that first minute and twenty seconds or so that had elapsed before Mr. Fix-it picked up the tape recorder. That sound, like a crash of thunder, was loudly recorded, but after another few seconds the rest was silence. While he had not touched the microphone itself, whose little button was still in the "on" position, what he had apparently done, in tapping and fussing with the recorder itself, was cause the main switch, above the cassette receptacle, to snap back from "play" to "stop," thus rendering academic the question of whether the mike was left switched on or not.

I had to console myself with the thought that the tape I had made of that morning's dress rehearsal with Hymowitz was at least an exact duplicate of what we had played tonight, and was still intact.

Later, however, by an odd fluke, I accidentally erased the same portion of the first movement of the Nardini from the dress-rehearsal tape, so, to have one complete record of the perform-ance with Edwin Hymowitz, I had to rerecord, from one machine onto another, by use of an ingenious patch cord that permits direct transference of recording from the tape on one machine to that on another, the sole surviving fragment of the actual concert tape, in order to piece out the accidentally erased beginning portion of the dress-rehearsal tape.

As the rest of the program went on and I sat and watched and listened to the other performers, I was amused by the irony that, of the four who played that evening, I alone, the one amateur, had undertaken to play "virtuoso style," without notes. The other three, all pros, calmly set up music racks and blithely proceeded to read from scores, without a care in the world. This could have been because they were called upon to play on such short notice, after the only other amateur entry had had to be scratched.

As for the evening's fund-raising aspect, the only money received by the orchestra that was directly attributable to this project, which obviously cost the Relins a pretty penny, amounted to hardly more than petty cash. I told the only two women over whose presence there that evening I had any control that the price of admission was a hundred-dollar contribution to the New York Orchestral Society. They both believed me, and sent in checks in that amount. Then, ashamed of myself for having perpetrated such a barefaced put-on, I thought the least I could do by way of amends was pretend to believe it myself, and as evidence, in case the matter ever came up again, I sent in a check for the same amount. The rest of the attendance, so far as I know, paid purely in applause, which was all they were asked for.

At that, I was undoubtedly the evening's only big winner. Aside from the dubious distinction of being able to say that I had played the violin in public, or, anyway, practically public, at a hundred dollars a seat (including my own, a detail that didn't necessarily demand disclosure), I got a direct dividend out of that concert that I have been cashing in on ever since. For I got a new fiddling partner out of it, to fill another morning with music before work each week, along with a chance to play a dazzling and ever-changing assortment of the greatest violins and bows in the world.

In other words, while I didn't literally die that night, as at one point I was prepared to believe I actually had, in a figurative sense I did, for I went from there straight to a sort of fiddler's heaven, because no less a term is adequate to characterize the vaults at Rembert Wurlitzer from seven to nine on a Thursday morning, which is where I've been ever since.

ELEVEN

ee Wurlitzer, who carries on the business of her late husband Rembert, came to my recital with two young couples, her daughter Marianne with her husband, Gene Bruck, and Charles Ponall, with his young and pretty and pregnant wife, Catherine.

Charles Ponall is young himself, to be a veteran of concertizing both here and abroad, as he was when he was brought in to the great fiddle firm to organize and run the subsidiary known as RW Service & Supplies, Inc., the separate string and supply department. This may sound involved, because it is, as Lee Wurlitzer's second husband, Heinrich Roth, aside from doing a large business in orchestral instruments, out of Cleveland, is also the American representative for the peerless Pirastro strings.

I thought none of this was of any particular interest or concern to me at the time, because I had no way as yet of knowing that Lee Wurlitzer's coming to that silly concert with those two young couples was to be the fusion point of my whole fiddling

LEE WURLITZER AND HENRY HOTTINGER
Lee Wurlitzer electrified the fiddle world with her purchase of the Hottinger collection for a million dollars in 1965. Hence this exchange of million dollar smiles.

Rembert Wurlitzer, Inc.

mania, bringing the two halves of my passion together for the first time in over fifty years.

Always before, my fiddling time and my collector's interest in the violin had been, if not entirely separated, at least conducted on alternating current. My fiddling had been done on violins hardly worthy of the name in the high appraisal standards of the connoisseur of the instrument; and such expression as I had ever been able to give my collector's instinct had been confined largely to books and to the occasional sight of rare instruments in exhibitions, behind glass, or in circumstances where I would not have presumed to lay playing hands on them. That was why the rare exception to the rule, in the case of Rafael Druian's Nightingale Strad, had been such a red-letter occasion for me.

And even after the acquisition of the Gudgeon had led me to try to bring about some betterment in the relative estrangement of these two sides of my interest in violins, it was still a very rare occurrence for me to get so much as a look at another Strad.

To anybody but another fiddle fan this may not sound like such a deprivation. But I am hooked on fiddles as another might be on drugs, and there are times when I wonder which, in the long run, might prove the more costly habit to maintain. You and I might sympathize with another's dependence on drugs, but we could never begin to comprehend either the agonies or the ecstasies that he undergoes.

So it may be with any attempt to communicate feeling for violins. You either have it or you don't. If you do, I don't have to tell you what the sight and the touch and ultimately the playing embrace of a fine fiddle feel like. And if you don't, though your taste be exquisitely refined and you may be knowledgeable in any number of the arts, there is probably no other way I can convey a feeling for it than to hand it to you. And even then, as Dr. Johnson says, unless you play, yourself, you "can do nothing with it" but hand it back again.

And yet, there must be more to it than this, for what can you "do" with a painting, for instance, or a Cellini cup, or almost any other object of art that you can name? Well, yes, a Cellini cup—I suppose you could drink out of it, but it would be tantamount to putting a horse like Man o' War to work delivering a milk route.

Anyway, for those who do see violins as objects of art worthy of admiration on the highest level, there is no more beautiful sight on which to feast the eye. Not the light through a Vermeer window, not the blue of Veronese sky, nor the flame of a Turner sunset can be any more majestic than that play of light on maple through the varnish of a Stradivari's back.

And today this sight is nowhere in the world to be seen any more often than at Rembert Wurlitzer.

That was not always true. Once upon a time, when I was knee-pants high, there were actually more priceless violins to be seen at Lyon & Healy in Chicago, though that was before Wurlitzer got Jay C. Freeman away from them. And in those days, too, W. E. Hill & Sons in London had many more than they have today.

Rembert Wurlitzer, Inc.

The balance of ownership has long since shifted across the Atlantic, and that means that today Rembert Wurlitzer is the crossroads for Cremonas that Hill was for so long in the past.

That's why my ears pricked up at something Charles Ponall said that night at the Relins' when we were all standing around after the concert.

What he had said first was something about the trill I had sustained before the final harmonic in the Kreisler *Liebesleid* with which I had wound up my part of the playing. Something about "quitting winner" or "quite a climax" or any one of a number of things like that, and beyond making an acknowledging moue or muttering thanks I hadn't paid much attention to it, because compliments are only adumbrations of small talk like remarks on the weather.

But he went on to say something apropos of what Joe Eger had mentioned in introducing me, about the early bus I took from Jersey, to get into town in time to fiddle in the office from six-thirty until eight. He said that, as the victim of the train and tube schedule, he couldn't get in from Jersey quite that early, but that he could make it by seven or with luck by ten of, and would I like to play some duets down at the shop, where they had "some terrific fiddles."

Wow. I knew what some of those fiddles were, though I had only once been in there, a couple of years before, on the occasion of Simone Fernando Sacconi's seventieth birthday, which they celebrated with a big loan exhibition. There were superb violins and bows there from all over the world, but I had taken pains to notice that the greatest of them were their own.

We settled on Thursday, the morning after my lesson with Mr. Shub, when my fiddling could be assumed to be at its best, as the best day to begin this venture of two souls' journeys among masterpieces.

Charles brought out of the vault two fiddles and two bows, and, while I looked at them, he went to fetch, into the front room where we were going to play, a double music stand with racks back to back. This front room at Rembert Wurlitzer is itself a shrine of fiddledom, and along two of its walls are long tables on which instruments can be laid out. On one of these rested the Duport Stradivarius cello, which, while Charles went into the vault, I saw, recognized, and went over to examine. It has since been sold for a record price—well above that hundred-thousand-dollar mark that no violin has yet reached.

On the walls are pictures of Ysaye, of Ole Bull, of Heifetz, Mozart, and Beethoven, and a small picture of Rembert at his desk, examining a fiddle. Across the front of the room, where the windows are, is a small "fence," like a courtroom railing, behind which there is a desk, placed like an artist's, to get the full benefit of the north light. Here Dario D'Attili, as general manager, customarily sits by day, although there is also a space still reserved for him in the workshop on the floor below.

Into this room Charles brought, that first time, the Goding Amati of 1662, a fiddle I had known from pictures since my boyhood but had never actually seen before, and the Salabue Francesco Stradivari of 1742, the most perfect example of the work of the elder of the master's two violin-making sons. Violins signed by either Francesco or Omobono are rare. They were both old men by the time their father died in 1737 at the great age of 93, and neither long survived him. In this Francesco, and in the Antonio that afterward came to be known as the Messiah, because Tarisio kept promising for so long to bring it to Vuillaume in Paris but could never bring himself to do so, Count Cozio di Salabue had two of the most perfectly made and preserved violins ever to bear the magic name of Stradivarius. Salabue was the first great collector, buying from Paolo Stradivari, the merchant son, ten Strads that had been left in the master's workshop at the time of his death, and owning as many as a hundred in all, at one time or another. He was also a dealer, for whom some commission-house brokers fronted, to spare a nobleman the onus of directly engaging in trade, and he actually employed J. B. Guadagnini as his personal violin maker. But although he was amassing fiddles for the last quarter of the eighteenth century, he was actually vending them for the first forty years of the nineteenth, and at his death in 1840 supposedly had only one fiddle left, a Nicolo Amati.*

The Goding Amati, which I picked up first, and tried with the plainer of the two bows, is beyond all doubt one of the three or four greatest violins Stradivari's master ever made, and it was such a delight to play that I actually never even touched the Francesco, although its beauty is blinding, until another day.

Of the two bows, the one I had picked up first is a Tourte, and you would pass right over it in a case of fancier bows. The other that lay beside it that first morning of our duets is an exhibition bow by Lamy, all gold and filigree, and on subsequent trial a splendid example, too, of "handsome is as handsome does."

But in all honesty I must record that I forgot I had a bow in my hand at all, as long as I played the Goding Amati that morning.

Since then, this has become a standing joke. Whenever I can't remember what bow I have been using with whatever fiddle I've been trying out on a given morning, it invariably turns out that the bow in question was a Tourte.

If style is indeed the absence of style, so that the greatest is the

* Alas for legend, of which fiddle literature is so largely made up, this often-quoted story of the man who had once owned a hundred Strads only to wind up with one Amati turns out to be merely a fraction of a half-truth. According to the Cozio manuscripts, as translated into English by Ettore d'Attili, Salabue's cabinets, as inventoried at the time of his death in 1840, still contained, instead of that "one Nicolo Amati," forty-eight violins by his "house maker" J. B. Guadagnini, along with two Guadagnini violas and two Guad cellos, and seventeen other violins as follows: a Jacobus Stainer of 1665, a Duher (Stainer pupil) of 1656; a "German violin varnished black," a Zenta of Turin (labeled Nicolo Amati); two violins by Andrea Guarneri, of 1658 and 1679; three Giofreda Cappas, one unlabeled, one labeled Andrea Amati 1647 (although Andrea Amati died in 1611), and one labeled Nicolo Amati 1683; a Gatto (without label), a Guarnerius *filius Andreae* of 1707, a Francesco Rugeri il Per of 1684, a Pietro Guarneri of Mantua labeled 1722 (he died in 1720); two Carlo Bergonzis, of 1731 and 1733, a violin attributed to Andrea Amati, and a violin attributed to G. B. Rugeri, labeled Girolamo Amati, son of Nicolo, and dated 1729. A total of sixty-five violins, and yet, as recently as 1942, the knowledgeable expert J. C. Freeman, in contributing a chapter to John Fairfield's *Known Violin Makers*, told, in all good faith, how Count Cozio was down to his last Amati when he died.

MOZART ON A PAIR OF GUADS (7 A.M.)
Ole Bull eavesdrops.

Hermann Kessler

one that you are the least aware of, then the genius of François Tourte is beyond compare. With a Tourte, and this has proved to be true not only of that first one but of several others since, I simply can't remember—that is, I am never consciously aware of —having a bow in hand at all. Obviously, the Tourte becomes so much a part of me that its very existence is for the duration of the playing time completely eclipsed.

This is something I have never yet been able to say of a violin, though I have found myself saying, of several Strads, "This fiddle almost seems to play itself." In fact, that is the way I felt about my own little Gudgeon the first time I ever had it in my hands, and still feel about it whenever I pick it up, after playing no matter what great Guarnerius or other fiddle of first magnitude.

But despite the heels-over-head infatuation that I felt for the Goding Amati, that first morning Charles Ponall and I began playing together, an even greater thrill, after we had settled down to trying some duets, was the realization that here again I had found that same solid prop to my own shaky game that I had first experienced when I felt my tennis being bolstered up during a game with John Hennessy.

Though only in his thirties, Charles is a veteran of playing with symphonies, beginning with violin and later adding viola. He plays with that rock steadiness that is less unusual with orchestra men than with soloists, and from the start I found him giving me a sense of the beat that none of my exasperated teachers had ever in my life been able to hammer into me, hard as they tried.

Within a very few sessions, putting most things on tape even as we sight-read our way through them, we had done the Mazas and Viotti violin duets, the Pleyel duets for violin and viola, and the Mozart Viennese sonatinas for two violins and, not long afterward, we were doing the Bach Concerto for Two Violins as I could never even have dreamed of doing it back in the days when I played at it with Linda Denby in Chicago on the two Klozes.

IN THE ROOM WHERE WE PLAY
Dario d'Attili has just come in after a duet session and is explaining to Charles Ponall and me why this 1742 Del Gesù couldn't have been made in 1734.   *Hermann Kessler*

To be sure, there is an equally enormous difference between playing on two Klozes, however mellow, and being able to match up pairs of Strads or Guarneris or even, as in one combination I remember with special affection, the Baron Knoop Petrus Guarnerius of Venice with a viola by Gasparo da Salò that must have been a good four hundred years old but swelled the walls of that front room at Rembert Wurlitzer like a cathedral organ.

Pietro Guarneri of Venice is a maker esteemed almost as many notches below his uncle of Mantua, whose namesake he was, as he is below his much more famous brother Joseph of Cremona, the peerless Del Gesù. But here, as with the Salabue Francesco, was a case where you can forget the labels and just relish the works. No rose by any other name was ever savored more appreciatively than that Baron Knoop Peter of Venice during the weeks I played it, when there were Strads and other ostensibly much greater Guarneri on hand to pick from, and I was sorry when it left, to find a home with a collector in the Azores.

It's remarkable how quickly you can develop either an antipathy or a genuine affection for a fiddle. That Petrus of Venice, though I played it only a few weeks, is a violin I'll die loving, although I doubt that I will ever see it again, but the Ernst Strad of 1725,* incomparably higher in the ranking of the world's remaining store of great violins, is a fiddle I put down after a few bars, to pick up instead, and to keep on playing, a Petrus of Mantua of the first decade of the eighteenth century.

The Ernst is a virtual twin of the Portuguese Strad, their backs and sides having quite evidently come from the same slab of maple, although the Ernst's is a one-piece back. Its varnish is near miraculous, and it was one of the two favorite solo instruments of the famous Heinrich Wilhelm Ernst. But I much preferred, during the time they were both in the Wurlitzer vault, the Grun of 1714, now known as the Kneisel, and presumably to be known in some future time as the Sanford Allen, ex-Grun, ex-Kneisel, which is an ugly duckling when placed beside the Ernst.

* Not to be confused with the Ernst Strad of 1709, which is better known and more often listed. The great fiddlers, like Joachim, got their names on many instruments, because several of them traded with dealerlike frequency.

The fame of the performers in whose hands they have been is a factor, along with beauty and state of preservation, in putting up the premium on some violins above others that might outsing them if these factors were to be completely disregarded. The trouble is that, being so subjectively lodged in the mind and eye of the beholder, these factors can't be disregarded, which makes for some relative bargains, even today, among great violins.

For one thing, the Ernst is too treble for my taste, too effusively soprano, although, speaking of subjective factors, I can recall not liking a Gasparo da Salò violin on the very ground that it was not treble enough. The thing I loved about a Gasparo viola was the thing that grated on me in a violin of the same origin.

Generalizations are probably as unreliable in this field as in any other, but in general it does seem to work out that the fiddlers fall into two broad main categories—those who have a natural affinity for the Strad, and those who haven't, but love the Guarneri. The division is about as accurate, say, as the division of mankind into introverts and extroverts, with the former preferring the Strad and the latter the Guarneri.

You can't say that the Strad is small and the Guarneri large, because actually on measuring you'll find more Strads going over fourteen inches and more Guarneri coming under that much of the full-size norm, but because of the vigor of the model and the Brescian-pointed sound holes, Guarneri tend to look larger, and Strads smaller, than they measure. Nor can you say that Strads are more feminine (I recall David Sackson's perceptive remark about "the growl of a Stradivari," though I suppose it could be said that a lioness growls, where a lion roars) than the Guarneri are, because the forms are essentially alike, except that the Guarneri do tend as a rule to look much more burly than the Strads.

Some few great players, such as Paganini, Kreisler, and Heifetz, rose above this division, and played both Strads and Guarneri, although in each instance with one of the latter as special favorite.

One thing you can argue, beyond all risk of being subjective about it, and that is scarcity value, because there are more than twice as many authenticated Strads as there are Guarneri del Gesù.

Another thing that seems to me to be demonstrable in the instruments themselves is that the Strad and the Del Gesù represent the culmination of two distinct and parallel schools of development of the violin, with the former standing as the crowning glory of the direction given by old Andrea Amati in Cremona nearly two centuries before, and the Guarneri as the similarly logical ultimate realization of the possibilities inherent in what was begun by Gasparo da Salò in Brescia at about the same time. Toward this polarization of the great Italian violins into two kinds, it seems to me you can safely assign most makes of the great days, with fairly few exceptions. Carlo Bergonzi, for instance, you would as naturally put in the line running from Gasparo to Del Gesù as you would put Giofreda Cappa into that running from Andrea Amati to Antonio Stradivari. This device of using the Strad and the Guarneri as magnets around which to cluster the rest is fouled up here and there, of course, by the persistence of such makers as Gabrielli of Florence and Techler of Rome in adhering to the Stainer line.

And fiddlers, as a rule, I venture, would divide just about as naturally as the instruments themselves do, toward whichever group best meets their own instinctive predispositions.

Out of my mornings with Charles, for instance, I have pretty well found my experience of playing many fiddles tending to support my own initial feeling to class myself as an Amati-Strad man. By the same token, I feel fairly sure that if Harry Shub had been there with me, Thursday after Thursday, his own preferences would have shown him to be a Gasparo-Guarneri type.

With only one outstanding exception to date, I find I tend to hate the highly vaunted late Del Gesù violins, of the last lustrum of his life, the years just before and just after the famous Paganini Cannon of 1743. The Dragonetti and the Jarnovic, for example, both of this period, I found harsh and hard and shrill, and so unresponsive, as compared to almost any Strad I have touched, that getting out the great tone that I know is in them seemed to me to be only comparable to a high-forceps delivery.

Given this inclination, not to say prejudice, on my part, I have been delighted to find some Guarneri among my Thursday morning loves. Only one Del Gesù, true, but two Peters, one of Mantua and one of Venice, and one Joseph *filius Andreae*, of all of which I could say as I played them on different mornings, separately and together, along with John Gay: "Oh how happy could I be with either, were t'other dear charmer away."

Shub's mind obviously runs on different tracks from mine. After each of my mornings with Charles, when I would start to talk about different fiddles at my next session with Mr. Shub, he would immediately ask, "How much is that one?" and almost never had it occurred to me to find out. I would have to make a mental note to ask Charles to find out from Dario the next morning.

To me the wonderful thing about the Thursday mornings with Charles has been from the beginning that here was a chance to enjoy the finest examples of a great art form, without ever having to entertain any of the mundane thoughts and feelings of envy and greed and guile that are a part of all commerce, even in the realm of beauty.

It is as if, for two hours every week, all the rules, moral and legal, that ordinarily both govern and shape our lives, were momentarily lifted. We don't have to buy anything, decide anything, I almost said marry anything, and perhaps in that doubtless Freudian slip of the pen is the unwittingly uncovered but truest analogy to this weekly orgiastic occasion of ecstasy.

We both love fiddles—I, who say so to everybody who will listen, including the traffic cop on the corner, and Charles, perhaps even more, because he has actually done what I only verbalize, in changing his line of work, the better to be with them all the time.

Now as for you, I've got to assume that you at least aren't allergic to fiddles, as I sometimes think my Janie must be, or otherwise I'd be at a loss to understand why you're here. (Ever since my mother died I've had to recognize that I have no completely constant reader.)

But let's say, just for the sake of argument, that you're not so queer for fiddles as you are for women.

So, toward a more perfect understanding, let's just suppose for the moment that what Charles and I are up to every Thursday morning from seven to nine is dalliance not with the greatest fiddles of the last three centuries, but with their greatest women. And grant us, too, simply for the purposes of analogy, an ability to pick up and play one as easily and as often as the other. (I have already pointed out that all the normal rules, both moral and legal, that govern and shape our lives, have been providentially suspended for the magic hours of seven to nine on Thursday mornings.)

Now, Charles comes out of the vault, not with this lovely and perfect J. B. Vuillaume of 1869, but with, instead, the Empress Elizabeth of Austria, purely by coincidence, you understand, because he can't possibly know how I've suffered with unrequited love for her shade since I was nine, and for himself he brings, not that stately and majestic Gasparo da Salò viola, but Catherine de Medici, of approximately the same time. I have to say approximately because the viola is not as specifically dated as she is.

Picture us then, lolling at our ease with the likes of these, and can you imagine anybody having more fun without laughing?

Or, if the evocation of these two does nothing to your salivary glands, Charles can go back into the vault and bring out, not the fiddle that was made for *le Vert Gallant*, Henri IV, by the Brothers Amati, but, instead, his queen, Margaret of Navarre, who would at least broaden the conversation in every sense, if her *Heptaméron* is to be taken as any sort of sample, and, instead of the Andrea Amati made for Charles IX, bring out Diane de Poitiers, whom you've remembered so vividly all these years

180

from the Clouet portrait of her, at Chantilly, pensively fondling the left nipple.

But enough of such idle fancy. I'd actually much rather talk about the fiddles.

My own one notable exception to my general dislike of the later Del Gesù models is a 1742, which, oddly enough, at one point in its career, was listed and certified as of the year 1734. Tonally I would have found that easier to believe, as this fiddle has all the dulcet smoothness of a great Strad but backed by all the power that only a late Del Gesù is supposed to possess. But Dario D'Attili, who knows as much about these matters as any man now alive, has taken me on a point-by-point tour of this fiddle's entire construction and shown me, in detail so minute and so multitudinous as to be overwhelmingly convincing, that this Del Gesù couldn't have been made more than at most a year or two before the date it now bears, and that it is inconceivable that it could have been made anywhere nearly as early as the date that was once wrongfully ascribed to it.

DARIO IN THE VAULT

Rembert Wurlitzer, Inc.

SACCONI IN THE WORK-
SHOP
*Rembert Wurlitzer,
Inc.*

Dario, as both maker and judge of violins, would of course defer
to Simone Fernando Sacconi, under whom he has literally grown
up over the past thirty years. But, although I would give Sacconi
full marks as the genius everybody concedes him to be—he repaired a broken peg on my Gudgeon so skillfully that no jury
could possibly determine which of the four pegs it was—still a
much bigger dividend for me, that has also come indirectly out
of my Thursday mornings with Charles, is the extent of the
wonder that Dario has wrought by adjustment of three of my
fiddles, giving them a tone in each instance that I never dreamed
they possessed.

For the Gudgeon he did the least, simply because there was the
least to be done, physically, to realize its maximum tonal effectiveness. It will never fill Carnegie Hall, in any case, although,

after my own experience with it in my one public appearance in the concert at the Relin's, I am convinced that in the right hands it could. And that was before Dario adjusted it. Now I'd bet on it—though naturally not in my hands—to fill the Hollywood Bowl or the Yankee Stadium.

But an even greater change was wrought in my Amati. That fiddle, which had at first enchanted me with its big tone, did not wear well, as over the course of a couple of years it came to seem increasingly harsh and hard. I felt that while the hands were obviously the hands of the Brothers Amati, as showed in every line, the voice was coming to seem more and more the voice of Nicolas Lupot. Though the volume was all anybody could ask for, and in fact was such that after the first little while I never again played it without a mute, I was bothered by an insistent metallic acerbity—you could almost say a tinniness—that I have always associated with French fiddles, as contrasted to the almost-liquid limpidity of the true Italian tone.

Although he kept it for weeks, and had to make a new bridge and sound post, and even tinker with the bass bar, Dario finally passed a small miracle by way of de-frogging it, so to speak, and the true voice of Cremona was again to be heard in the land, or at least in those portions of it that I infest.

He did almost as much for my Stainer, which had received no adjustment of any kind since Rosenthal had endowed it with its new top, more than two years before.

Here again, he had to put in a new bridge, and tinker even longer than he had with the Amati, before he was satisfied that he was at last getting out everything that was in it, and by the time that point was reached, after more than two months, that fiddle, too, sounded better than any almost-Stainer has any right to sound.

I would never have believed that adjustment could make such a day-and-night difference in the sound of a violin, if Dario had not proved it to me three times over. I thought I had had adjustments before, away back when I was a boy, and had to send my student fiddle from Grand Rapids to Hornsteiner in Chicago, an action roughly tantamount to sending a combination can opener and knife sharpener to Cartier for repair, and other people over the years had from time to time done things to try to ameliorate the tone of the Kloz, but Dario invested the word "adjustment" with a totally new dimension of meaning for me.

Charles says there's only one other man he knows who can begin to do what Dario can do with a violin, and that's Hans Weisshaar out in Hollywood; but for me the world of improvement in a fiddle's tone is bounded on the east and west by Dario's two hands.

As a result of Dario D'Attili's ministrations, three out of four of my fiddles now bear the name of Wurlitzer on their bridges, with only the Gudgeon still faithful to its provenance and wearing the name of Moennig there. To this extent, the Amati and the Stainer are sailing under false colors, as their old bridges read "Moennig" and "Rosenthal" respectively. As for the other one—the third violin that says "Wurlitzer" on its bridge—that's a fiddle that hasn't been mentioned before, for the simple reason that it is another story entirely.

suppose you could best liken it to a case of never having had the least intention to marry the girl, but look
at us now.

Thursday after Thursday Charles and I played with those great
fiddles, many of whose names—the Rode Strad, for instance—
are next to legendary in violin annals, and week after week I
would play on one to which I had become particularly attached,
for as long as it was still in the house.

For example, I played the Kneisel Strad for a month's worth of
Thursdays before it left Wurlitzer's hands, and it had reached the
point where, concentrating on the intricacies of some of the
duets we were doing, I would forget which fiddle I was playing,
almost to the extent that I always forget which bow I'm using,
or indeed that I have a bow in my right hand at all, which I have
now come to accept as the surest sign that it's a Tourte.

But it is seldom true, and never to be taken for granted, that any fiddle will stay that long. This is probably as good a gauge of the affluence of our society as any, when you stop to consider that the prices of most of these fiddles begin about where Rolls-Royce prices end, with a round twenty-thousand figure turning out to be somewhat less than average. I would have thought that at those prices the violins would stick around the shop a lot longer than they do.

Frequently a fiddle will be there for the first time one Thursday and be already gone the next. This was the case with several Strads and a couple of Del Gesùs. As I recall, I didn't regret the going of either of the Guarneri, and felt that I had hardly had time to manifest any meaningful mourning for the passing on of any of the Strads.

The departure of the Kneisel, I must admit, gave me something of a pang, but I was quickly consoled because every week something wonderful would come along. I had the Scottish University Strad in my hands only one Thursday, for instance, but that was such a heady infatuation that in my memory it is now on a pedestal practically on a parity with that of the Kneisel. The Goding Amati and the Baron Knoop Peter of Venice are both long gone, of course, but I will always remember them with great affection. And yet it would never have occurred to me, even after prompting by Mr. Shub to find out "what they want for that one," to have thought about acquiring either. But that's the great thing about these mornings with Charles—they are totally free of these mundane considerations of "getting and spending," but are dedicated instead to sheer and unalloyed enjoyment.

Usually, just by way of trying to exercise my eye for a fiddle, I will sing out what I think it is, the minute Charles brings a fiddle out of the vault, and before I have had a chance to examine it at all closely or to look at its label. Except in such obvious instances as a Strad or a Del Gesù or a Gasparo, where it's almost hard to be wrong, my average is apt to be, like that of those ESP card tests that they conducted so long at Duke University under Professor Rhine, something that is best measurable against the percentages of pure chance.

One morning, for instance, when Charles brought out a mellow old yellow fiddle of familiar shape, I shouted "Brothers Amati" with all the certainty of a sailor sighting his home port.

Wrong! I was as incredulous as if I'd just mistaken the identity of one of my three sons.

"No," said Charles, "Petrus Guarnerius of Mantua."

I couldn't believe it. The curve and design of the sound holes, the sharpness and pitch of the pointed corners, the antic grace of the scroll—above all, the golden yellow of the varnish and the height of the arching, top and back—everything about this fiddle said nothing other than the Brothers Amati to me, and having lived with one for over two years I thought that was the make that, next only to Stradivari, I knew best. But the label confirmed (as if Charles wouldn't know and labels couldn't lie) Petrus Guarnerius Cremonensis, and sure enough, it was Mantua, 1702. Not even seventeenth century, and I had all along thought that I could at least guess which century a violin came out of, based on what I had always thought was a pretty good eye for the age of wood.

When I played it, however, I heard and almost felt a sound such as I have never had out of any other violin before or since, except that 1742 Joseph del Gesù which is the one exception to date to my general dislike of the later Guarneri. Like that, this had not at all what I would have expected from a Brothers Amati, but what I might well have expected from the biggest of Strads, a dulcet smoothness and hair-trigger responsiveness, but combined with a solid sense of tremendous resources of reserve power.

I don't know quite what I had expected, as I knew hardly anything about Peter of Mantua violins, never having even seen more than one or two, and never having played any before this. I would have said I was strictly a *filius* man, when it came to the Guarneri side of the fiddle street. I had played several *filius Andreae* specimens over the course of the past forty years or so, and had always found them much more to my taste than the much more vaunted violins of his son Joseph del Gesù. As for those of *his* brother, Peter of Venice, I had as I have said played the Baron Knoop with great pleasure. But as for those of his uncle, Andrea's other son Peter of Mantua, I had really nothing to go by.

I found myself playing this Petrus of 1702, however, not only that Thursday, but the next three as well, giving it up only for the Scottish University Strad of 1734, on the one Thursday Charles brought that out of the vault. That day Charles played the Petrus, while I played and raved about and generally made a big fuss over the Strad.

It was after I had played back our tape of that morning, and Charles had gone back to the other end of the shop to make us some coffee, that I picked up the Petrus from the long table where he had left it beside the Scottish University Strad and started to play the Nardini on it.

Charles, coming back along the hall toward the front room where I was playing, said,

"Wow, that fiddle really does sound, doesn't it?"

He was assuming, of course, that I was still playing the Strad, about which he had left me babbling when he went away to make coffee.

"Wrong fiddle," I said, "that was the Petrus."

I told Mr. Shub about it at my lesson the next week, and he said:

"I don't know whether you realize it or not, but you know you've talked about that Petrus more than about any other single violin of all those you've been playing down there. I think you must be falling for that fiddle more than you know."

And then, of course, he wanted to know, as always, how much they wanted for it.

I thought in citing the fact that I didn't even know, after all these weeks of playing it, that I was giving the best possible

PETER D'ATTILI MEETS PETRUS OF MANTUA
Dario d'Attili, who is so devoted to Petrus of Mantua that he named his son after him, attempts to show the boy the reason that he should be impressed with such an honor.

Rembert Wurlitzer, Inc.

proof that I was no more serious about this particular violin than I had been about any of the others, or indeed expected to be about any of them, no matter how many we played on our Thursday mornings.

"I've always had a secret yen for a *filius*," I said, "I guess for no better reason than if I had one I could feel I'd squared the circle, or boxed the compass, of the four great makes, Stradivari and Guarneri, Stainer and Amati."

"Well, I suppose a lot depends on how much it is," said Mr.

Shub, "but I think I'll make it a point to drop in there and have a look at it before I go."

He was leaving ten days later on a European concert tour, and I would be having only one more lesson before he left, so when I got back to the office I called Charles to find out how much the Petrus might be, in order to tell Mr. Shub the next time I saw him.

Charles thought it was twenty, but asked me to hang on a minute while he checked with Dario to make sure. When he came back on he said yes, it was twenty, and that Dario had said it was the finest Petrus he knew and that he was pretty sure that a collector coming in from Chicago the next week to see it, along with a couple of other fiddles, would pick that ahead of the other things he had to show him.

I was a little surprised that it wasn't more money than that, remembering that the Baron Knoop Peter of Venice had brought even more than that, and always having understood that the Venetian Pietro's prices were away below those of his Mantuan uncle.

Still, I had known, about the Baron Knoop and about the Goding Amati, before they were actually sold, both what they were expected to bring and at least where, if not exactly by whom, they were being considered, and in neither instance had the news been of more than casual significance to me. It had been about like discussing whether it would or wouldn't rain.

But suddenly I felt a surge of jealousy about this new suitor for one of "my" fiddles. The others had meant less than nothing to me personally, but now all of a sudden this sinister unknown from Chicago made me see red.

As I had explained to Shub, I didn't really expect to "marry" any of these fiddles I fondled and enjoyed week after week, so I was puzzled to see how personally I was taking this news about what was after all still only a pretty vague threat of invasion from the west, which might or might not result in the carrying off of the Petrus.

So I tried to concentrate on some rather urgent work I had to do, involving a deadline that was already past, and thought I would forget about the fiddle. But after working awhile with half a mind on the job, I found myself talking to my broker, something I hadn't done in the better part of a year, and what I was talking to him about was the possible nature and number of bits and pieces of white paper he would have to sell for me to raise, well, say, for instance, around twenty thousand dollars.

As I did this, I heard a small stern voice from somewhere within telling me what a fool I was to be taking steps like these before I really knew anything about the fiddle. I didn't even know, for instance, whether it had a name, whether it had a Hill certificate or not—

Telling the broker I'd call him back, it suddenly seemed more important that I find out the answer to these embarrassing questions from my conscience. I didn't know the answers, but it was as simple as calling Dario to find out.

No, it didn't have a Hill certificate. Hmm, twenty grand for a fiddle that lacked what my Strad had, at some forty percent less than that, indeed that my Cappa had even had (remembering Miss Warren of Deal) at twenty percent of this violin's price.

"As a matter of fact, it's interesting," Dario said, "that this violin has been in and out of the hands of the Berlin dealers, Hammig & Co., almost as long and as often as your Amati was with Caressa and Français, in Paris, never really going anywhere else."

Yes, my Amati had gone somewhere else, leaving Caressa & Français with Pierre Vidoudez and following him back to Geneva. But what about a name, did this fiddle have any one special one, such as Lady Tennant and Erna Rubinstein for my Strad, or Vieuxtemps for my Amati?

"Well, that's even more interesting," Dario said, "because the one name of any importance that's connected with this Petrus is a very important name—Franz Schubert—"

"What!" I interrupted, "I never knew that Schubert had the price of a plate of porridge—"

"Exactly," Dario resumed, "and of course it's a different Franz Schubert. This one was Wagner's concertmaster at Bayreuth in 1869."

Oh. About like having something that belonged to William Shakespeare, only it turns out to be William H. Shakespeare, another fellow.

So I was more surprised than ever to find myself talking to my broker again after that.

As much money as I had paid for the Strad, the Amati, and the Stainer, plus the three Dodd bows too, if you allow for the fact that the Kloz had never really cost me anything (and that is, of course, the way collectors habitually reckon). And for what, I asked myself sternly.

For an almost-Amati, if you want to look at it that way, since that is what I had first taken it for, and equally apparent that that is what old Petrus of Mantua must have had in mind, if not actually before him, when he made it. Just another old yellow fiddle, in effect, but not even as old as any of the other three, if you follow Rosenthal's dating of the Stainer as 1659 and not Gabrielli's of almost a hundred years later. Certainly not as old as the Strad of 1672 or the Amati of 1618, and, despite the beauty of its one-piece back, really no better looking than any of them.

But alas for the admonitions of the small voice from within, the next actual voice I heard was my own, telling the broker to go ahead and sell, though not telling him why, as would have been only natural ordinarily, since he's an old friend.

But why not? I asked myself back. Why not sell a few pieces of
paper that my old man slaved and sweated to acquire, only to
leave me when he got hit by an unwary lady driver? I'd rather
leave a few pieces of wood, as artfully put together as these were,
if any day now the same thing should happen to me. Besides, the
scarcity value of these particular pieces of wood, as joined by
Peter of Mantua over two hundred and fifty years ago, is a lot
greater than that of any pieces of paper, inflation being what it
has already become.

I don't even know whether the fellow from Chicago ever actually came that next week or not, or whether he bought anything
if he did.

I only know that something made me rush to buy that Petrus as if my life depended on its acquisition.

Why, after scores of other fiddles, Thursday after Thursday, had failed to move me to make so much as the bat of an eyelash, I should have thrown myself headlong at that one, I can't explain, any more than I can explain why a salmon, as I have often seen, will ignore scores of flies moved artfully past his lie, never according them so much notice as the flick of a fin, and then suddenly throw himself at one as if it represented his last chance in the world, as indeed in almost every case it does.

Lukas Foss has a phrase: "Making love to the past." It could serve as any fiddle fancier's most fitting epitaph. It's what Charles and I do, really, every Thursday morning, and I suppose it's akin to what some people do Sunday mornings in church. I'm sure there are more worthy pastimes, though I can't think of any that seem to me more rewarding.

Hobbies, as such, should not be rewarding, or at least not enriching, to oneself, save in enjoyment, lest they cease by definition to be hobbies. Still, I suppose there are valid instances where some men, through activities pursued with only a hobby interest, have made riches either for themselves or for others. A stamp collection, I understand, put together by a hobbyist of the early nineteen hundreds, would have soared by now to a value far higher than any conceivable collection of stocks and bonds he could have put together at the same time. And forgetting the monetary aspect, I can think, right in this field of fiddle fancying, of a couple of instances where things done only as hobbies are bound to rebound to the benefit of all the other hobbyists in the field, like Herbert K. Goodkind's years of collecting of data and pictures to form his *Iconography of Antonio Stradivarius*. This will be of great interest and worth a hundred years from now, when your activities and mine will long have ceased to matter. The same is probably true of the endless measurements and calculations that were made over the years by Alexander Sved, a Hungarian-born American dentist who died out on Long Island a couple of years ago in his seventies. He had been an engineer before he took up dentistry, at which he became conspicuously successful, but from boyhood he had been fascinated by fiddles. So he spent his spare time, through several decades, in attempts to formularize the ideal proportions of the Stradivari model, based on his measurements, and consequent engineering calculations, of scores of specimens. This conceivably could be of both interest and value, generations from now. He even went so far, at the height of his Strad study, as to make a dozen fiddles himself, all in one year, 1944—a rate of production that even professionals might envy.

Some men in this field, from as far back as Cozio di Salabue and Tarisio to Rembert Wurlitzer and Bill Moennig in our own time, have been so dedicated to the violin that it dominated their lives to a degree encompassing hobby and passion, vocation and avocation, so as to blur any possible line of demarcation between where one left off and the other began. But they represent the end-point of hobbyism as war represents the end-point of politics.

My own modest pursuit of this hobby over these last thousand days has been more like playing a game, to the degree that within that time-span I first acquired fakes, or at any rate copies, and then subsequently original examples, of the four seminal makes of the violin, the Stradivari, Stainer, Amati, and Guarneri. With the acquisition of the Guarneri I could really consider this aspect of the game finished, the circle squared, the compass boxed. More or less the same thing could be said of the fiddlesticks as of the fiddles, as within a week after I had first fallen for the Guarneri Mrs. Rosenthal came up with a Dodd bow (probably by John Kew's father, Edward Dodd) that at last matched my memory of over fifty years—one with that primitive form of frog, lacking both plate and ferrule, with the hair on the underside of the frog exposed as in double-bass bows and some cello bows, that I had thought, and then finally begun to doubt, that I remembered. That turned my trio of Dodds into a quartet, and a lovely sight they make, racked up in the lid of one of those new superlightweight Hill double cases, with the Gudgeon and the Petrus cradled in the fitted apertures below them. (Rafael doesn't envy me this one; in fact, he goes so far as to agree with W. C. Retford that this Dodd *is* obsolete, though I play it with joy, finding it fairy-light in the hand.)

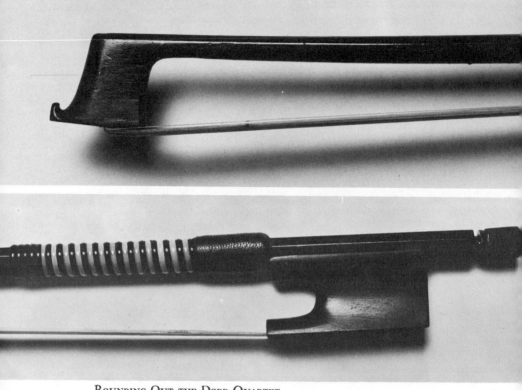

ROUNDING OUT THE DODD QUARTET

Henry Wolf

To reach this end-point of at least one aspect of this hobby, the game-form of the collecting side, has cost me some fifty thousand dollars, give or take a couple of hundred, in just about three years or, in round numbers, fifty dollars a day. What the hell, a good psychiatrist would have cost as much and what would I have to show for it today, besides which I can remember only one experience where a psychiatrist actually said, "Goodbye, Bub, you're on your own now," after as short a time as a mere three years. That was the lady psychiatrist who discharged my old friend Howard Baer, and what she said was something to the effect of, "Throw away the water wings, from here on you sink or swim on your own." For the rest, though many are good friends of mine, I'm afraid that visiting them is like studying Latin—all you seem to get out of it is the necessity of studying more Latin.

In contrast, after my latest foolishness, the mad rush to snatch the Petrus out of the hypothetical grasp of the putative seducer from Chicago who was supposed to be coming to look at it the next Tuesday, my broker called me the other day to say, apropos of nothing at all, that he didn't know or care what I had done with the twenty-two thousand I had got out of him in late May by the sale of some of the stocks I had from my father, but he just thought it would interest me to know that if he had tried to sell them for me now he'd have been lucky to get as much as fifteen thousand for them.

So when I broke down at long last and told him why I had wanted those stocks sold at that time—to get the Guarneri and the fourth Dodd bow—he said:

"The Lord's supposed to protect fools, drunks, and children, and it sounds as if you must have been carrying coverage in all three categories. I hate to talk against my own business, but quite frankly I think you're better off, as a hedge against inflation, with what you've got than with what you had."

Whether that should prove to be true or not, the fact does remain that after these thousand days I still have the fiddles and the bows, and I have had more fun, in both their acquisition and their enjoyment, than I can imagine getting otherwise on anything like fifty dollars a day and being left, at best, only with memories of pleasures past.

Of course I can't take them with me, I know, but even that side of it can be a source of satisfaction and pleasure. For instance, while I was still in the first state of bemusement at the thought of actually owning a Stradivari, and before I had acquired the other three fiddles that form the cornerstones of my little collection, I willed the Strad to Marlboro College in Vermont, for no better or worse reason than that I have been very much impressed by the concert series, "Music from Marlboro," and because I was pretty sure that when I left it to them, for the use of deserving students who couldn't afford a good fiddle, the bequest would be an unusual and even exciting event for them; whereas, if I left it to some such obvious place as The Metropolitan Museum of Art or the Library of Congress, the most likely reaction that I could expect to elicit would be the polite equivalent of a yawn, as getting another Strad would be nothing either new or very memorable to either of those august institutions. (The Metropolitan has several, and the Library of Congress has not only the Whittal quartet, including the incomparable Betts Strad of 1704, but also Fritz Kreisler's bequest.) My poor little Gudgeon would have been small potatoes there.

As it was, the president of Marlboro College wrote me back in precisely the terms I might have expected, his letter beginning, "Wow! Nothing like this has ever happened to us before. . . ."

All that it has meant since then is that I have felt an added sense of responsibility and stewardship, overlaid upon my ownership of the Strad, that I don't feel for any other fiddle. I have never since then taken it on a plane, or even on a cruise. I can't forget the two Strads that perished with Jacques Thibaud in that Alpine plane crash, nor can I forget the hanged-man look of the Monster, Lundberg's Maggini copy, the morning I was tuning it up on the *Raffaello* between Naples and Genoa and the neck suddenly went *skew-gee*, bending away over to one side in response to the pull of the strings as the glue gave way under a sudden atmospheric change produced in the wake of coastal storms.

I don't say that the collecting aspect of my enjoyment of the violin is necessarily over, though it would seem to have achieved a certain sort of completeness with the replacement, or rather the supplementing, of my first four auction fakes with the subsequent four original specimens. Maybe it has, and maybe it hasn't. (Even contemplating the question poses the thought that there is still one copy, Lundberg's Monster, the presumably Mathieu copy of a sixteenth-century Maggini, and the mouth does water at the thought of one of those mellow old yellow fiddles with the rusty double purfling, the inner row of which is so gracefully looped both at top and bottom of the back, such as the one Maggini I saw so long ago in the hands of Frank Stewart in Grand Rapids, and getting one of those would raise my present odd number of nine to a nice round even number like ten.)

Even aside from that more or less logical occasion to supplement, rather than supplant, one of my present cherished store of fiddles, I recognize that I don't have a "real" Guadagnini, for instance —either Lorenzo or J. B.—instead of the purported but utterly unauthenticated "Antonio" of Turin, 1851, nor do I have a Gagliano, the make that Bill Moennig is so enamored of, and seems to regard as the real "sleeper" among the Italian master violins of the second rank.

Given money enough and time, I can see that there would even be some fun, from time to time, in getting a few fiddles whose makers' names had the same initials as my own.

Let's see . . . there's Andrea Guarneri, of course, and there's Alessandro Gagliano (just last week with Charles I played four of them, one right after the other, and one really was lovely), but no matter.

There's fun enough, for the rest of my days, simply in playing the fiddles I have, even if I were not to buy so much as a new sheet of music, from here on out. If I were rationed to one tune, I could live with the Adagio from the Third Mozart Concerto in G, K216, along with its Franko cadenza, and feel there was room left for all my potential growth as a fiddler, however hard I practice from now on. For nothing serves to underline, so challengingly, Goethe's phrase about the inordinate length of art and the relative brevity of life as that most rewarding and most maddening, that most exciting and least forgiving, most exacting and most bewitching of all man's playthings, of all his objects of art, indeed of all his demons, that most animate of all inanimate creations, the violin.

APPENDIX I

(All photographs in the appendices, courtesy of Rembert Wurlitzer, Inc.)

THE ANATOMY OF A VIOLIN

The 30 Locations of a Violin's 92 or 93 Parts

1.	top (table or belly)	2
2.	back	1 (or 2)
3.	upper bouts	2
4.	middle bouts	2
5.	lower bouts	2
6.	sound holes	2
7.	linings	12
8.	corner blocks	4
9.	upper block	1
10.	lower block	1
11.	neck	1
12.	pegbox	1
13.	scroll	1
14.	pegs (tuning)	4
15.	fingerboard	1
16.	nut	1

17.	strings	4
18.	bridge	1
19.	tailpiece	1
20.	tailpiece gut	1
21.	E string tuner	1
22.	saddle (under tailpiece)	1
23.	tail pin	1
24.	bass-bar	1
25.	sound post	1
26.	label	1
27.	purfling	36
28.	chin rest	1
29.	button (base of neck)	
30.	pegs (back and belly)	4

Total   92   (93)

Note 1: Numbers in parentheses on instrument shown on page 200 indicate locations of parts not visible.

Note 2: Upper left-hand picture, opposite, shows intermediate stage of achieving modeling of the top's arching (out of a solid block of spruce). Right-hand picture shows inner side of top with sound holes cut and showing bass-bar.

Note 3: (*a*) Lower left-hand picture shows back with sides in place and linings and corner blocks in position. (*b*) In right-hand figure, open trench on upper left side of back shows space for insertion of the three separate strips of purfling (outer two black, inner strip white). (*c*) Button, at top of back, is shown square, before rounding off to follow contours of base of neck, when latter is fitted.

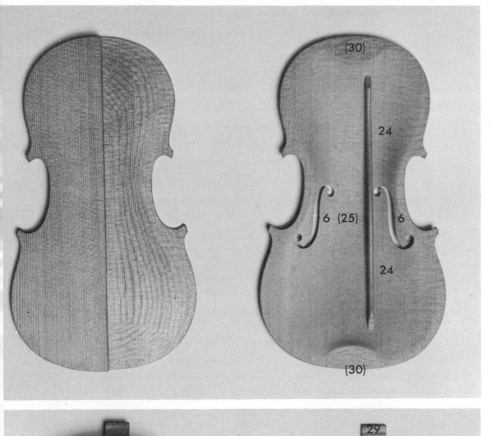

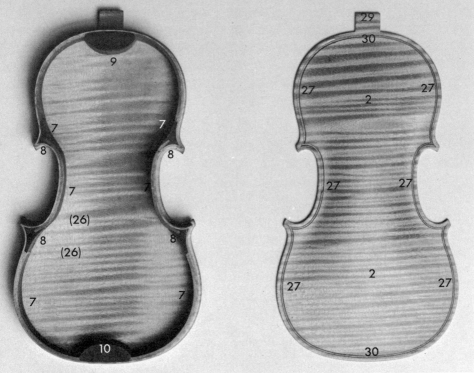

APPENDIX II

THE CHANGING STANDINGS OF THE FOUR SCHOOLS

The Relative Values of Stainer, Amati, Stradivari, and Guarneri Instruments in 1700, 1800, 1900, and Today

Today you could say that the four makes are ranked with Guarneri and Stradivari at nominal parity, with Amatis commanding half their price, and Stainers not much more than half the price of Amatis. This is an almost exact reversal, as far as the Strads and Guarneris are concerned, from the relative price situation that prevailed in 1800, when even a Del Gesù commanded half the price of a Strad, and an almost exact reversal of the relative price positions of all four makes another century earlier. In 1700, Stainers and Amatis enjoyed the near parity, with Strads commanding less than half their prices, and with the Guarneri not yet in the running.

In the summer of 1969 a modern record for a Stainer violin was set in a sale at Sotheby's, at £1350, or roughly $3,250. This is less than a fourth the going price for a prime Nicolo Amati today, and a far cry indeed from that time, already ancient history when reported by Sandys and Forster a century ago, when a Stainer violin brought "half the price of Pittsburgh."

Of course, in the infancy of the violin, an Amati was the fiddle of the royal and princely courts, and Andrea Amati's was an unrivaled name that was accepted widely as a virtual synonym for the Cremona violin. Early in the seventeenth century, Cremona violins were priced better than two to one over those of Brescia, on which the former were regarded as a great improvement and refinement.

With the Amatis as virtually the only makers whose name was generally known, it is a little hard to understand, from this remote point in time, how the ascendancy of the Stainer began as early as the mid-sixteen hundreds, unless it is because the Stainer early became the choice of soloists, whereas the Amatis were more favored for sets of instruments for the various courts. Certainly for the hundred years from 1680 to 1780 the ranking violins were the Stainer and the Amatis, with the former ranked ahead of the latter more often than not.

Perhaps the best single indication of how firmly the Stainer was enthroned is found in the listings of Count Cozio di Salabue.

Writing *after* 1800, this pioneer of the great collectors of Cremonese instruments wrote: "The best violin makers are: Giacomo Steiner (sic) of Switzerland; Castagnery and Chapuy of France; Andrea Antonio and Nicolo Amati, Stradivario Antonio, Guarnerio and Rugeri of Cremona. There are also other good makers who built passable violins. They are: Albano Mattia, Horil Giacomo and Tekler David of Germany; Galliani Nicola of Naples, and an unknown peasant from the territory of Ascoli in the Marca of Ancona, who for the excellence of his works, made exclusively by virtue of his admirable genius and his other personal qualities, deserves that his name be transmitted to posterity, Giuseppi Odoardi. He died recently, at the age of about 28 years only, after he had made with his own hands as many as two hundred violins, many of which some years from now will probably not be second to the best Cremonese makes."

That the man who had owned a hundred Strads, including the Messiah itself, should still have accorded first place to "Giacomo Steiner of Switzerland," mentioning "Stradivario Antonio" only seventh (and J. B. Guadagnini, whom he employed for twenty years, not at all), may seem incredible, but it certainly helps us understand today how powerfully the Stainer once held sway.

Throughout the 1680–1780 period, too, the Stainer and Amati models were overwhelmingly preferred, as the pattern to follow, by violin makers everywhere. Even such a gifted maker—and soloist—as Pietro Guarneri of Mantua—who must have had first-hand knowledge of all the violins of Cremona in his youth, not excepting those of Stradivari, which had so strongly influenced his brother, Joseph *filius Andreae*—nevertheless clung by obvious preference to the Stainer-Amati arching for all the violins he himself made.

While no one player could have turned the tide in Stradivari's favor, still there is no question but that Viotti, in the seventeen eighties in Paris and in the seventeen nineties in London, precipi-tated the general swing away from the Stainer-Amati high-arched model to the flatter Stradivari for solo use. This swing was a quick one, and by the first decade of the nineteenth century there was a really sudden craze for Stradivari, with makers as well as players quick to affect the formerly neglected flatter Stradivari. This trend was given further impetus after the eighteen twenties, by the sudden rise of the hitherto unesteemed Del Gesù to near parity with the Stradivari, after which time the dominance of the latter two flatter models was never again challenged.

By following the prices given at different times in widely scattered sources in fiddle literature, it is possible to chart the rise of the four schools of violin design, and the fall of the first two, over the last three centuries. Short of feeding all the data thus gathered into a computer, a simple averaging of the many prices cited at various periods over this time-span gives a pretty accurate long-term picture, although its exact accuracy could well leave something to be desired at given points along the way.

But leaving out such dubious peaks as "half of Pittsburgh" for the Stainer and the wrongly rumored $125,000 for the Dolphin Stradivari, it is nevertheless fairly easy, by sticking to cited prices of actual records at the different times, to get a pretty good idea of how Stainer and Amati prices started above and then fell below those commanded by Stradivari and Guarneri. Obviously, what this can neither picture nor allow for is the exceptional price paid for the exceptional instrument, then or now.

But here is how the various value patterns graph out, based on this simple method of picturing them. What they give is an accurate picture of the changing relative values over the span of almost three centuries. What they cannot possibly give, in view of the constantly changing purchasing power of money over such a long period, and particularly in view of the continuing and virtually universal inflation since 1914, is any truly accurate indication of "how high is up," in attempting to compare today's prices with those paid for the same instruments in the past. In view of this, it is better to consider the rating points, from one to forty, purely as relative and comparative units, indicative of a scale of desirability, rather than trying to treat them as monetary units, in anything like an exact relation to today's dollars. Today, when a Lupot can be insured for ten thousand dollars, and the same sum may be refused for a Tourte bow, it is foolish and futile to try to say exactly how much a Strad that sold for ten thousand dollars in 1914 is worth—or will be, a year or two years hence. That particular Strad is worth whatever it will bring, depending on its owner's luck, and the auctioneer's aptitude, and the economic conditions—and mood—that may prevail the next time it is put up for sale.

Certainly a Cremona violin will, within the measurably near future, cross that hundred-thousand-dollar mark that has heretofore been crossed only by the cello—and it could well be any one of a dozen Strads. But the odds are slightly better that it will be a Del Gesù. There is one additional factor at work, and this one is not a variable, like those cited above. It is scarcity value. There are fewer than half as many known Del Gesùs as there are Strads—and, for that matter, under a tenth as many Peter of Mantua fiddles—so the odds will inevitably and increasingly favor the Guarneri, even though, as many believe, Stradivari deserves to be the unrivaled name. One straw in the wind: at Sotheby's on November 27, 1969, a Peter of Mantua, 1715, set a new record for a violin other than a Strad or Del Gesù sold by auction.

207

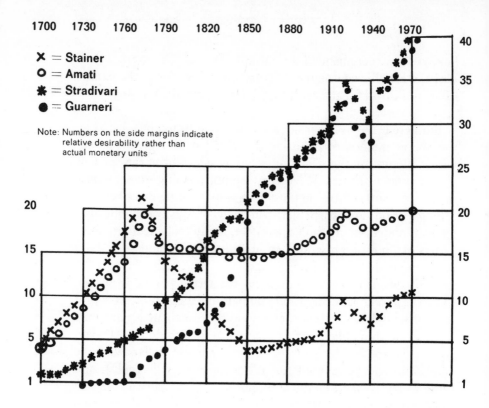

Writing after 1805, Count Cozio of Salabue revised his earlier listing, to accord both Antonio Stradivari and his son Francesco first rank among Cremonese makers, along with the Amati family of makers and, in fact, right behind his first choice, Stainer. As for the Guarneri family, he appraised them as makers of the second class in the school of Cremona and said that in doing so he was following "the generally accepted list." He gave Andrea Guarneri and both his sons, Pietro and Giuseppe, equal standing. About Del Gesù, however, whom he characterized as a nephew of Andrea, he had some reservations concerning all but his earliest works, saying that "most of the instruments he made afterward, though he used the same patterns, hardly place him in the third category."

With this sublime irony we are brought full circle, or soon will be when, as almost inevitably will happen, one of the late Del Gesù violins, undoubtedly one made after Stradivari's death in 1737, will break new high ground in the steadily rising and now vaulting valuations of Cremonese instruments.

APPENDIX III

SOME OF THE VIOLINS MENTIONED

A Gallery of the Famous Instruments from the Vaults at Rembert Wurlitzer, Inc.

The Goding Amati, 1662. With its pedigree intact back to the time it came over the mountains from Italy to Paris in a bag on Tarisio's back, and bearing the same name since 1857 when it was part of the collection of the English pen maker James Goding, this violin, by Stradivari's master, Nicolo Amati, was recently sold by Rembert Wurlitzer, Inc., and established a record price

for this make. Made in Amati's sixty-sixth year (he died in 1684 at the age of eighty-eight), it is typical of his Grand Pattern, but unusual in its state of preservation, even the back of the scroll showing almost no sign of wear.

The Baron Knoop Guarneri, 1743. This is the undoubted masterpiece of the Venetian Pietro Guarneri. Normally held in lower esteem than the works of his more famous uncle, Peter of Mantua, in this one instance Peter of Venice leaped over his head, to approach the stature of his Cremonese brother, the peerless Joseph del Gesù. Even in the collection of Baron Knoop, who had a quartet of Strads, this violin was outstanding. Playing it is an unforgettable experience.

The Kneisel Strad, ex-Grun, 1714. This was willed by Franz Kneisel to his son in 1926, and later acquired by Rembert Wurlitzer. Kneisel had it from his master, the Hungarian, Jacob Grun. Tonally, this is one of the great Strads.

The Salabue Francesco, 1742. This violin, by Stradivari's eldest son, is as remarkable for its virtues of construction and tone as for its state of preservation, and would be outstanding in any

collection. The scarcity of labeled works by either of Stradivari's two violin-making sons, and the fact that they were so over-shadowed by their father's fame, kept either of them from ever attaining the master ranking that might more readily have been accorded them under any other name. This specimen, perfect both as work of art and as instrument, made by Francesco Stradivari in his seventy-second year, fittingly honors the name of Count Cozio di Salabue, the first great collector of Strads.

The Lord Norton, 1737. This violin changed hands in England as often as Le Chant du Cygne in France, and is considered by many experts, both there and here, to be even more deserving of recognition as Stradivari's last masterpiece. Marianne Wurlitzer, who literally grew up with Strads, has more affection for it than for any other of the hundreds she has known.

The Swan Song, 1737. Assumed to be the master's last work,

ever since Tarisio brought it to Paris in 1825, this is one of the most frequently copied Strads. On an inscribed slip beside the label, Stradivari noted his age as his ninety-third year. This instrument was sold in Paris in 1870 for the near equivalent of £200, and bought by David Laurie for £500 nine years later. By 1886 it was sold for twice that, again in Paris, hence the persistence of its French name, Le Chant du Cygne. It has been in this country since 1925, when it became a part of the famous Wanamaker collection.

The Earl of Falmouth Bergonzi, 1733. Looking more like a Strad but sounding more like a late Del Gesù than most of Carlo Bergonzi's violins, the one Bergonzi attribute that is unmistakable here is the characteristic breadth of the scroll. With an illustrious history, it has been a part of many important collections, most recently that of Henry Hottinger. The beauty of its one-piece back is noteworthy.

The King Stainer, 1659. The height of its arching no more pro-

nounced and no less graceful than that of the Goding Amati, this perfectly preserved specimen gives an inkling of why Jacobus Stainer's is the only non-Italian name ever mentioned in the same breath with those of the masters of Cremona. There is no proof that he ever worked in Cremona, but his were the only Teutonic violins ever to give rise to such a supposition. The dragon's head in lieu of the customary volute of the scroll is carved of pear wood. The King was part of the famous Hottinger collection.

The Dolphin Strad, 1714. (So named for the striking figuration of its back, the evanescent sheen suggesting the play of the sun on a dolphin out of water.) Bought by George Hart for £200 in 1868 and sold by him to John Adam for 600 guineas in 1875. Acquired by Richard Bennett for 1000 guineas in 1882. First owned by Hills in 1892 and sold by them to Munro (characterized by Henley as a "Lieutenant in the Royal Navy") and reacquired by Hills in 1950, when they sold it to Jascha Heifetz. Widely rumored, and even reported in a number of news media in 1967, as "the first hundred-thousand-dollar violin," purport-

edly having been sold well above that price to "a West Coast syndicate." Like the old story about the fur business in St. Louis, it wasn't the West Coast and it wasn't a syndicate, and it wasn't even a hundred thousand dollars. It was measurably less than that figure. Subsequently the Duport Strad Cello was sold for measurably more than that figure. Lee Wurlitzer knows exactly how much more, and how much less, in both instances. But when the stakes become astronomical, success in the brokerage of Cremona treasures, like that in poker, seems to have a certain bearing on the ability to keep the eyes open, the face straight, and the mouth closed.

The Hellier Strad, 1679. The Hellier is the second of Stradivari's ornamented violins, preceded by Le Lever du Soleil of
1677—perhaps named the Sunrise for the luminosity of its amber
varnish. Ten of these ornamented instruments are known today.
This is one of the few Strads known to have been purchased by
Hill & Son, literally, at "second hand," as it came to them in 1884
from the estate of Sir Samuel Hellier, Wimborne, where it had
been kept since its purchase, direct from Stradivari in Cremona,
by Sir Samuel himself for £40 in 1734. This sum was over three
times the master's usual price. Its size is large for an early Strad.

The Duport Strad Cello, 1711. Rated by the Hills at the beginning of the century as the foremost of their list of the twenty

Strad cellos they considered the best, the Duport now holds the record as the highest priced single work of the master. It began life at twice the price usually paid him for a cello, Stradivari having made it on special order, with that explicit understanding, for a doctor in Lyons. Duport, who was the teacher of the Prussian King Friedrich Wilhelm, paid 2400 francs for it before the turn of the nineteenth century, and it has been setting record prices ever since. Passing to Duport's son in 1819, he sold it in 1842 for ten times the price his father had paid, and a record price was set again in 1892 when the Hills acquired it for Baron Knoop. Nobody knows how high the price of a Strad can go, but it is safe to assume that the Duport cello will remain the best means of finding out.

L'Aiglon Strad, 1733. This quarter-size violin is still known by the name first given to Napoleon's son, the boy King of Rome, for whom it was once intended to be a gift. The long neck and large pegbox dwarf the body, giving that resemblance to an eaglet, straining upward from the nest to be fed, that makes its diminutive name singularly appropriate. Variously attributed to 1733 and to 1734, the master was turning ninety when he made this exquisite toy.

The Urso Del Gesù, 1742. Tonally unique among the later Guarneri violins, this instrument has all the clarity and responsiveness of any Strad, but supercharged by the tremendous thrust of power that only a late Del Gesù possesses. This violin was once certified by a New York dealer as being a work of the year 1734 (in Kreisler's heyday it was generally felt that the later fiddles were inferior, an assumption that has since been reversed). It came to this country as the solo violin of Camilla Urso, at which time it had a scroll by Daniel Parker. The present scroll, as shown here, is the work of Dario d'Attili.

The Scottish University Strad, 1734. This is one of the great
sleepers among the master's finest productions. Less well known
than others of comparable excellence, it is overlooked in Henley's
listings, and accorded too brief mention in Doring's. Kept out of
circulation for a long time by the circumstance that provides its
name, this fiddle, like the Camille Urso Del Gesù, embodies a
virtual crossbreeding of Strad and Guarneri tonal attributes. The
clarity and ease of articulation of the early Strads, combined
astonishingly with the trumpeting power of the later Del Gesùs,
give it an almost incredible range of expression, from whisper to
shout.

Alessandro Gagliano, Naples, 1709. An exceptionally fine example of the work of the first of a large family of Neapolitan violin makers, whose instruments have only recently begun to enjoy a greater vogue than they ever had in the past. With rare exceptions, such as the Guadagninis, dating variously from Parma, Turin, and Milan, and the instruments of "the mighty Venetian," Dominico Montagnana, violins made any appreciable distance from Cremona have always been at a discount, and particularly those from as far away as Naples. But this is a trend the Gaglianos have begun to reverse.

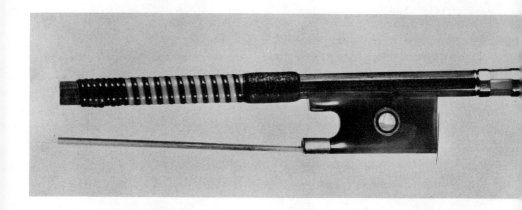

The "Priceless" Tourte, ca. 1830. This bow by François Tourte with tortoiseshell frog and gold mounting is the one for which Lee Wurlitzer has twice made news by refusing successive offers of ten thousand and of twelve thousand five hundred dollars, preferring to keep it in the Wurlitzer collection as one flawless example by the genius who is to the bow what Stradivari is to the violin.

The Petrus Guarnerius, Mantua, 1702. Mistaken for an Amati at first sight, this is the one violin of all the Thursday mornings that the author of this book, a confirmed Amati-Strad fancier,

found himself unable to give up. Made by Peter of Mantua, the uncle of the great Del Gesù and his brother Peter of Venice, this is one of some fifty violins known to be the work of this member of the great Guarneri family of makers. Leaving the workshop of his father Andrea to accept an appointment as court violinist in Mantua, he found that he enjoyed playing them too much to find time to make very many of them. No violas or cellos from his hand are known to exist, and his violins consistently follow the lines of those of his father's masters, the Amatis. This curious throwback on the part of a maker who was himself an accomplished violinist is unique in the long history of the Cremona violin.

Gasparo da Salò, Brescia. Bertolotti, known as da Salò, was long thought to be the "inventor" of the violin as we know it. But Andrea Amati of Cremona was his almost exact contemporary. Undated, but ascribable to the latter half of the sixteenth century, hence undoubtedly around four hundred years old, this instrument is remarkably well preserved. Primitive in comparison to the workmanship of a Strad, the sound holes nevertheless prefigure to an astonishing degree, by almost two centuries, those of the great Joseph del Gesù. The tone is somber, but of amazing vigor.

The Rode Strad, 1727. Not to be confused with the Rode Strad of 1722, which is the last made of the ten ornamented works of the master known to survive, this was another favorite fiddle of the early virtuoso, J. P. J. Rode, who was one of the first few, after his teacher, Viotti, to adopt the Strad for concert use. This violin has that greater breadth and intensity of tone which makes all Strads after 1700 incline more toward the Guarneri sound, to the same extent that it can be said that all made before 1700 lean toward the Amati tone. Outstanding exceptions to this generalization are to be found, of course, such as the Hellier of 1679 on the one side and the Scottish University of 1734 on the other.

The Ernst Strad, 1725. Here is another case where a violin shares with one or more other Strads the name of a great virtuoso of the past. (There are almost a dozen associated with Joachim, and several with Paganini and, nearer our own day, three with Kreisler.) This one, in hands as gifted as any of those mentioned, can be a very great fiddle, but it is one of the least forgiving of Strads in hands of less than stellar aptitude. Extremely treble, it sounds like a complaining wife, unless it is made content by consummate skill. The beauty of the maple wood that Stradivari used for about three years, from 1723 to 1726, had its price, and these Strads are for the vastly endowed, or the greatly daring.

The Jarnovic Del Gesù, 1741. As with the Dragonetti, to which it is of almost Siamese-twin closeness tonally, this is a great violin for those who are of the playing posture and temperament to get out the tonal treasure that is latent in the late Del Gesù violin. Primarily for a man, and a very assertive man at that, this fiddle will not meet you anything like halfway. Nobody could ever say of this, as is said of most Strads before 1700, that it "almost plays itself." You have to go in after the rich strong tone that is there, and you must be very sure of yourself to get it out without breathiness or scratch. Once you have accomplished this, the tone is of lusty splendor, and endowed with a giant's strength, but neither this nor the Dragonetti is a fiddle for the diffident or the effete.

The Dragonetti Del Gesù, 1742 (dated 1732 on label). Inevitably the fiddle sampler will find instruments that he under-appre-

ciates, along with others that he enjoys away beyond their due desserts. Forgetting monetary values, the author of this book wouldn't trade his cheapest auction fiddle, the "little red" bought for ninety bucks, for either the Dragonetti or the Jarnovic Del Gesù, if he had to retire with one fiddle to a desert island (a fate that some have recommended as a final solution to his fiddling obsession). This is not to suggest that either of the two late great Del Gesù in question is worth less than four hundred and forty-four times as much as he paid for the "little red," but simply to record the truism that a violin that might be superb for almost anybody else might not be right for you. Similarly, there might be high-strung race-bred cars that would be great for a Stirling Moss, but that you might crack up at the first corner. For a great enough artist this violin could be one of the greatest, esteemed as it has been since Dragonetti's day (1790s).

Giovanni Paolo Maggini, Brescia, early 17th century. Here is the real thing, to study in conjunction with the pictures of "The Monster," the purported Maggini shown in Chapter VIII. The Monster was made in France, probably toward the middle years of the nineteenth century, on the impetus of the great Maggini boom that was brought about by the fact that Charles de Bériot used a Maggini in public performances. There is a considerable degree of refinement of detail, as compared to the instruments of his master, Gasparo da Salò. And yet—despite the high praise accorded Maggini by the Hills—except for that brief moment in France, Magginis have never enjoyed the prestige of even secondary Cremonese makers. Shortly after Maggini's lifetime, Brescian violins were still bringing little more than a third of the price paid for those of Cremona. Here, too, however, the factor of scarcity-value will inevitably work to repair, in due course, four centuries of comparative neglect.

Gasparo da Salò viola, latter half of 16th century. Venerable as it is, it would be hard to find a more vigorous viola than this veteran of about four centuries of use. The original sides, carefully preserved, have been replaced, considerably altering the instrument's cubic air content, but the heroic proportions have otherwise been left unaltered. When teamed with a violin like the Petrus of Mantua 1702, or the Urso Del Gesù, or the Scottish University Strad, the effect in the second Mozart Duo, K424, is nothing short of glorious. What it would do for the Mozart Sinfonia Concertante K364 in the hands of a Hindemith, Primrose, or Trampler is something to dream on.

Now booming like an organ, now keening like a girl, it is hard to imagine a viola making sounds more beautiful than this. If nobody ever did anything for the cello after Stradivari, then surely nobody ever improved the viola beyond that point achieved by old Bertolotti at the very dawn of the illustrious history of the modern family of viols.

APPENDIX IV

A LIST OF PERTINENT ADDRESSES

For Those Interested in Playing or Collecting Fiddles

Amateur Chamber Music Players, Symphony Hall, P.O. Box 66, Vienna, Va. 22180

> A sort of Fiddlers' Anonymous—you get names to call up, wherever you may wander with your fiddle, so you'll always have somebody ready to play with you

Amati Publishing Ltd., 44 The Lanes, Brighton, Sussex, BN1 1HB, England

> Publishers of violin books, including the seven-volume *Universal Dictionary of Violin & Bow Makers* by William Henley

L. P. Balmforth and Son, 32–33 Merrion Street, Leeds LSZ 8LJ, England

> Violin experts; books, music, accessories

Mark L. Beard, Stradivari Studios, 51 Mundersley Park Road, Beufleet, Essex, England

> (Ceramic ashtray, dish or wall plaque, approx. *6″* × *5″*, choice of Fritz Kreisler, Nicolo Paganini, Henri Vieuxtemps [$5.00, U.S.A.])

Bearden Violin Shop, Inc., 6154 Delmar Blvd., St. Louis, Mo. 63112

> Violin makers and dealers

John & Arthur Beare, 179 Wardour Street, London W.1, England

Dealers and repairers of fine violins, violas and cellos since 1892 (Mondays to Fridays 9 A.M. to 5:30 P.M.)

Herman Bischofberger, 1201 E. Denny Way, Seattle, Wash. 98122

Violin makers and dealers

Blackwell's Music Shop, Holywell Street, Oxford, England

Music books and scores

Boston String Instrument Co., 295 Huntington Ave., Boston, Mass. 02115

Rare violins, repairs, restorations

Jack Brentnall, 2 Goldsmith Street, Nottingham, England

Specialists in old and modern violins

Broude Brothers Limited, 56 W. 45th Street, New York, N.Y. 10036

Reprints of books on violins and bows

Kurt Brychta, 921 Main Street, Buffalo, N.Y. 14203

Violin makers and dealers

Budapest String Shop, 6170 Michigan Avenue, Detroit, Michigan 48210

Violin makers and dealers

A. R. Bultitude, High View Cottage, High Street, Hawkhurst, Kent, England

Bow maker

H. A. Certik, 408 State Avenue, St. Charles, Ill.

Collector and dealer

Christie's, 8 King Street, St. James's, London, S.W.1, England

Fine art auctioneers since 1766

Karl Conner Violins, Poagston Arms Bldg., 532 W. Berry, Ft. Wayne, Ind. 46802

Violin makers and dealers

Cremona Musical Instruments, 320 Hayes St., San Francisco, Calif. 94102

Violin makers and dealers

Cremona Violin Shop, Jingu-Mae, 1–20–7, Shibuya-ku, Tokyo, Japan

Italian concert violins and cellos; French and English bows

A. David Dollin & Norman Daines, 45 Chigwell Rise, Chigwell, Essex, England

Restorers and dealers in rare violins, violas, cellos, and bows

Ealing Strings, 4 Station Parade, Uxbridge Road, Ealing Common, London W. 5, England

Restorers and dealers in fine violins and bows

Eastman Violin Shop, 281 Arkade, Cleveland, Ohio

Violin makers and dealers

Samuel Eisenstein, 140 West 57th Street, New York, N.Y. 10019

Violin maker and dealer

Otto Erdesz, 2307 Broadway, New York, N.Y.

Master viola maker

Sydney Evans Ltd., The Violin Shop, 49 Berkeley Street, Birmingham, England

Everything for player and maker

Everest Records, 10920 Wilshire Blvd., Suite 410, Los Angeles, Calif. 90024

Producers of *Four Hundred Years of the Violin*, an anthology of the art of violin playing, in a set of six records by Steven Staryk, playing the Camposelice Del Gesù, 1739

The Fiddle Shop, 3434 Edwards Road, Cincinnati, Ohio 45208

Violin maker and dealer

Emile Français, 12 rue de Madrid, Paris, France

Violin makers and dealers; successor to Caressa & Français, Gand & Bernardel, etc.

Jacques Français, Rare Violins, Inc., 140 W. 57th Street, New York, N.Y.

Son of Emile Français, of Caressa & Français, Paris

Max Frirsz, 130 West 57th Street, New York, N.Y. 10019

Violin makers and dealers

John Fullenwider's Violin Shop, 822 S. W. 152 Street, Seattle, Wash. 98166

Violin makers and dealers

Herbert K. Goodkind, 155 East 42nd Street, New York, N.Y. 10017

Compiler of iconography of Antonio Stradivarius: an index of Stradivari's production, planned for publication in '70

Gorisch Violin Shop, 3821 S. Sheperd, Houston, Texas 77006

Violin makers and dealers

Chester A. Groth Music, 915-919 Marquette Avenue, Minneapolis, Minn. 55402

Violin makers and dealers

J. P. Guivier & Co., Ltd., 99 Mortimer Street, London WIN 7TA, England

Violin makers and dealers

Prier Music Company, 144 East Second South, Salt Lake City, Utah

Violin makers and dealers

Hamma & Co., Herdweg 58, Stuttgart, Germany

Violin makers and dealers

Erwin Hertel & Son, Inc., 881 Seventh Avenue, New York City, N.Y. 10019

Violin makers and dealers

William E. Hill & Sons, 140, New Bond Street, London WIY OE5, England

Violin makers, repairers and experts (Mondays to Fridays, 9 A.M. to 5 P.M.)

Emil Hjorth & Sonner, Ny Vestergade I, Copenhagen K, Denmark

Violin makers and dealers since 1789

Willy Hofmann, 221 Argyle Bldg., 306 East 12th Street, Kansas City, Mo. 64106

Violin makers and dealers

Helmuth Keller, 1701 Walnut Street, Philadelphia, Penna. 19103

Violin makers and dealers

Eugene Knapik, Post Office Box 464, Chesterton, Indiana 46304

Violin maker, repairer, restorer

Ira B. Kraemer & Co., 626 Central Avenue, East Orange, N.J. 07018

Dealers and repairers of string instruments

C. E. Langonet & Son, 71 Brondesbury Road, London N.W. 6, England

Violin makers and dealers

William Lewis & Son, 7390 N. Lincoln Ave., Lincolnwood, Ill. 60646

Dealers in fine old violins

Littleboy and Son, 7 Sentry Hill Place, Boston, Mass. 02114

> Violin makers and dealers

Otto Luderer, 1514 Prospect Avenue, Cleveland, Ohio

> Violin makers and dealers

Lyon & Healy, 243 S. Wabash, Chicago, Illinois

> Musical merchandise

Merit Record Shop, 57 W. 46th Street, New York, N.Y. 10036

> Out of print violin records. Kreisler items a specialty.

William Moennig & Son, 2039 Locust Street, Philadelphia, Penna.

> Dealers in rare violins and bows, violas, cellos, master makers

Albert Moglie, 1329 F Street N.W., Washington, D.C. 20004

> Violin maker and dealer

Max Möller, 15 Willemspackweg, Amsterdam, Holland

> Violin maker and dealer

Music Minus One, 43 W. 61st Street, New York, N.Y. 10023

> Records of violin classics, with one violin part omitted—
> letting you be the soloist, accompanied by a full orchestra
> or chamber music group. J. Irwin Miller of Columbus,
> Indiana, plays either the Soil Strad or the ex-Isaac Stern
> Del Gesù to the accompaniment of these records all the time.
> Score of the missing violin part provided in a pocket in
> dust jacket of each record.

Frank Passa, 140 Geary Street, San Francisco, California

> Violin maker and dealer

Pearl Records, 56 Hopwood Gardens, Tunbridge Wells, England

> Recordings of violin virtuosi of the past

Placid J. Polsinelli, Gates Mills, 1785 S.O.M. Center Road,
Cleveland, Ohio 44124

> Violins, appraisals, and repairs (by appointment only)

Puttick & Simpson, Blanstock House, 7 Blenheim Street, New Bond Street, London W.1, England

Auctioneers of musical properties since 1794

R. W. Services & Supplies, Inc., 16 W. 61st Street, New York, N.Y. 10023

Separate accessories department of Rembert Wurlitzer, Inc.; also features books and phonograph records of interest to violinists and collectors (Tuesdays through Saturdays, 9 A.M. to 5:30 P.M.; summer, Mondays through Fridays)

William Reeves, Bookseller, Ltd., la Norbury Crescent, London, S.W. 16, England

Books on the violin, original editions, and reprints

Wilhelm Reidelbach, Maximilianstrasse 45, Munich, Germany

Dealer in new and old violins, violas, and cellos

Luthier Rosenthal & Son, 507 Fifth Avenue, New York, N.Y. 10017

Violin and bow makers to the world's leading artists

Paul Roth, 450 Quinton Road West, Birmingham 32, England

Violin maker, restorer and dealer

Philip Rubin, 1319 Eaton Avenue, San Carlos, California

Collector and dealer

Matthew Ruggiero, 40 Algonquin Road, Chestnut Hill, Mass. 02167

Violin makers and dealers

Salchow-Liu Associates, 1755 Broadway, New York, N.Y. 10019

Violin makers and dealers

David Saunders, 405 West Galer, Seattle, Wash. 98119

Violin makers and dealers

G. Schirmer, 4 E. 49th Street, New York, N.Y. 10017

Music Publishers, importers and dealers, publishers of Schirmer's Library of Musical Classics and *The Musical Quarterly*.

George Schlieps & Son, 881 Seventh Avenue, New York, N.Y.

Violin makers and dealers

Joseph Settin, 111 W. 57th Street, New York, N. Y.

Violin makers and dealers

Sid Sherman, 226 S. Wabash, Chicago, Ill. 60604

Certified master violins and bows

Sotheby's, 34–35 New Bond Street, London WIA 2AA, England

Auctioneers of musical instruments since 1744

The Strad, A monthly journal for professionals and amateurs of all stringed instruments played with the bow. Lavender Publications, Ltd., Borough Green, Sevenoaks, Kent, England. (Canada and U.S.A. $4 yearly)

The Stradivarius Association, 1170 Aubonne, Switzerland

International center devoted to Stradivari data. Membership $6.00 yearly

Stradivarius Violin Shop, 111 West 57th Street, New York, N.Y. 10019

Violin makers and dealers

D. W. Taylor, 10 Victoria Avenue, Hounslow, Middlesex, England

Violin bow maker and repairer

Paul Toenning's Violin Shop, 11340 Ventura Blvd., Studio City, Calif. 91604

Violin makers and dealers

Etienne Vatelot, 11 Bis, rue Portalis 8^e, Paris, France

Violin maker and dealer

Pierre Vidoudez, Corraterie 22, Geneva, Switzerland

Violin maker and dealer

Vitali Import Co., 5944 Atlantic Blvd., Maywood, Calif. 90270

Books on musical subjects

E. R. Voigt & Son, Ltd., Pellingbridge Farm, Scaynes Hill, nr. Haywards Heath Sussex, England

Violin experts since 1699

Kenneth Warren & Son, Ltd., 28 E. Jackson Blvd., Chicago, Illinois 60604

Violin dealers, makers, and repairers

W. D. Watson, Stebbing, Cheapside Lane, Denham, Bucks., England

Bow maker

Weaver Violin Shop, 1319 F Street N.W., Washington, D.C. 20004

Violin makers and dealers

Hans Weisshaar & Son, Inc., rare and modern violins and bows, 627 N. Larchmont Blvd., Hollywood, Calif. 90004

Expert repairs and appraisals, all accessories

Henry Werro, Zeitglockenlaube 2, Berne, Switzerland

Violin maker and dealer

Edward Withers, Ltd., 22 Wardour Street, London W1, England

Violin maker, dealer, and repairer

Cyril Woodcock, 49 The Lanes, Brighton, Sussex, BN1 1HB, England

Connoisseur and expert—rare violins

Rembert Wurlitzer, Inc., 16 West 61st Street, New York, N.Y.

Violin makers and repairers (Tuesdays through Saturdays, 9 A.M. to 5:30 P.M.; summer, Mondays through Fridays)

APPENDIX V

INSIDE THE SHOP

Workroom Scenes and Records,
Including "The Fever Chart of a Violin"

After four decades in the Wurlitzer Building on 42nd Street, Rembert Wurlitzer, Inc., moved in early 1970 to 16 West Sixty-first Street. In the new quarters are bigger and better vaults, more suitable facilities for the ever-expanding files which preserve, in minute detail, all the significant features of all the violins, violas, and cellos that have ever passed through this crossroads of Cremonese instruments, and—something for which room could never be found on Forty-second Street—a small museum.

Shown on the next two pages are pictures taken in the workshop that used to nestle beneath the main sales floor and offices, where the makers' and repairers' benches could benefit from the north light. The *genius loci*, Simone Fernando Sacconi, is shown in one view explaining a fine point of Stradivari construction to Marianne Wurlitzer; in another, looking out, for one of the last times, at the passing show of Forty-second Street. In the third photograph, general manager Dario d'Attili plays host in the workshop to a visiting member of the fiddle fraternity, Max Möller of Amsterdam, shown discussing a violin with one of the craftsmen who was just out of cameraman James Foote's viewfinder.

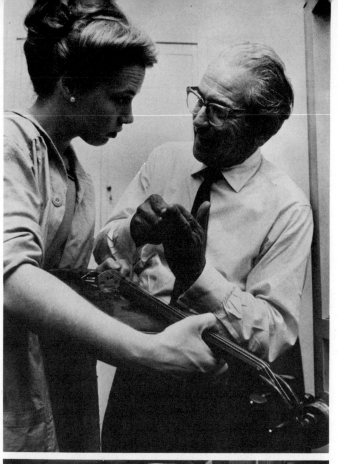

Shown on page 248 is a sample page from the binder in which case histories of the instruments are kept. In several instances, as with the Goding Amati, the ownership record goes back over a hundred and fifty years to Tarisio, and in one, that of the Hellier Strad, well over two hundred years, straight back to Stradivari himself.

Next, filled in simply to show how the record of an individual instrument's state of condition, preservation, and repair is kept, the repair chart that always follows a fiddle's registry page is in this instance devoted to a wholly supposititious violin. Just to give it a name, we could call it the work of those two other Brothers Amati, Fictitious and Anonymous. But it does show what even the most knowing expert cannot see, unless and until a violin is opened: the number and locations of patches, edges, and underlays. Almost all old violins have a sound-post patch and half-edges, the latter both as a result of, and to facilitate, the number of times the instrument must be opened, for purposes of conditioning and repair. But all other indications of cracks, patches, fill-ins, and replacements, as of blocks and linings, record the toll of age and use, or in some cases, accident and abuse. Hence this chart becomes, like a person's chest X rays or fever record, the most confidential part of the case history of an old instument, for it reveals as nothing else can the naked truth about that all-important factor, its state of preservation.

Registered Number   *Date Made*
(of Instrument or Bow)   *Maker's Name*   *City Made*

Label reads:

First known owner *City*   *Price*   *Date of Sale*

Other owner   *City*   *Price*   Date of Sale

Other owner   *City*   *Price*   Date of Sale

Last known owner *City*   *Price*   Date of Sale

Certificate   *Name*   *Date*

Magazine Article   *Date*

History Letter   *Name*   *Date*

Description:
Varnish:
Back:
Top:
Sides:
Model:
FFs:
Scroll:

Measurements:

Length   *Upper Bout*   *Middle Bout*   *Lower Bout*

FFs   *Ribs*   *Stop*

Remarks: *Date*
                                                           Initial

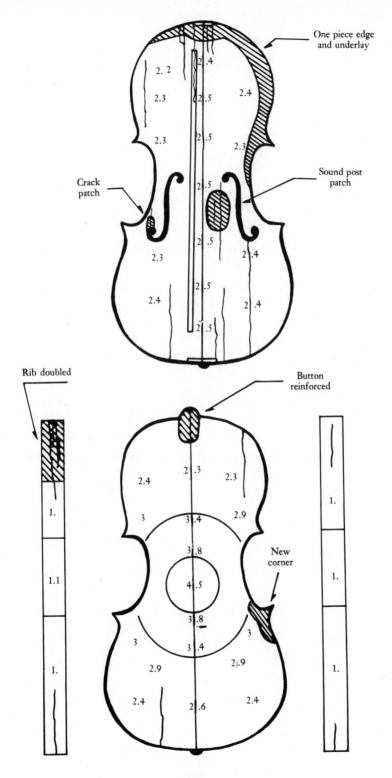

One piece edge
and underlay

Sound post
patch

Crack
patch

Rib doubled

Button
reinforced

New
corner

249

APPENDIX VI

GENEALOGIES

Charts Showing the Violin-making Members of the Four Families

AMATI

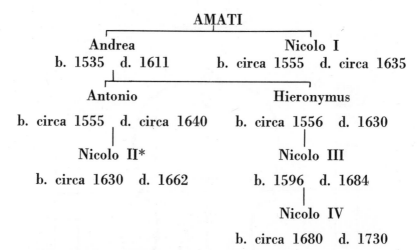

Andrea	Nicolo I
b. 1535 d. 1611	b. circa 1555 d. circa 1635

Antonio	Hieronymus
b. circa 1555 d. circa 1640	b. circa 1556 d. 1630
Nicolo II*	Nicolo III
b. circa 1630 d. 1662	b. 1596 d. 1684
	Nicolo IV
	b. circa 1680 d. 1730

* Andrea's brother, Nicolo I, and this son of Antonio were both makers of little importance. But the great Nicolo, master of Antonio Stradivari and Andrea Guarneri, is nevertheless referred to in violin literature as Nicolo III. (This is odd, considering that he was pushing forty before his short-lived cousin, Nicolo II, was even born.) The family name was spelled by Andrea, on some of his labels, with a "d" instead of a "t." There were two other violin-making Amatis, D. Nicolo of Bologna, circa 1700–1737, distantly related if at all, and Hieronymus II, elder son of Nicolo III, but the main makers of the Amati violin are those listed above.

STAINER

Jacobus
b. 1617   d. 1683

Jacobus Stainer really stands alone, unique among Germanic makers. He had a younger brother, Marcus, b. 1619 d. after 1680, who made similar but lesser fiddles, on a larger pattern. Otherwise few facts about him stand up, out of a large body of legend. He was copied, not only by German and Austrian and English makers, but even by many Italian makers, notably those of Rome.

GUARNERI

Andrea
b. 1626   d. 1698

Pietro Giovanni	Giuseppe Giovanni
(Peter of Mantua)	(Joseph *filius Andreae*)
b. 1665 d. 1720	b. 1666 d. 1739 or 1740

Pietro	Bartolomeo Giuseppe
(Peter of Venice)	(Joseph del Gesù)
b. 1695 d. 1762	b. 1698 d. 1744

Variant spellings: Guarnieri and Guarnerio. Older books made Del Gesù a cousin, but the relationship shown above was documented definitively by the brothers Hill in their monumental work on the Guarneri family in 1931.

STRADIVARI

Antonio
b. 1644 | d. 1737

Giacomo Francesco	Omobono Felice
b. 1671 d. 1743	b. 1679 d. 1742

Variant spellings: Stradivarto, Stradivario. (As for Stradivarius, that appears on the labels as Stradiuarius until 1729, after which it becomes Stradivarius.)

A SELECTIVE BIBLIOGRAPHY

BOOKS QUOTED, MENTIONED, OR
OTHERWISE OF INTEREST

Abele, Hyacinth. *The Violin and Its Story*. New York: Charles Scribner's Sons, 1905.

Applebaum, Samuel and Sada. *With the Artists. The art and techniques of violin, viola, and cello playing, as exemplified by Jascha Heifetz, William Primrose, and Gregor Piatagorsky*. New York: John Markert & Co., 1955.

Bachman, Alberto, *An Encyclopaedia of the Violin*. New York: Da Capo Press, 1966.

Baruzzi, Arnaldo. *La Casa Nuziale: The Home of Antonio Stradivari 1667–1680*. London: William E. Hill & Sons, 1962.

Bowen, Catherine Drinker. *Friends and Fiddlers*. Boston: Little Brown & Co., 1935.

Boyden, David D. *The Hill Collection of Musical Instruments in the Ashmolean Museum, Oxford*. London: Oxford University Press, 1969.

——. *The History of Violin Playing from Its Origins to 1761*. London: Oxford University Press, 1966.

Champfleury. *The Faïence Violin*. New York: Thos. Y. Crowell & Co., 1895.

Clarke, A. Mason. *The Violin and Old Violin Makers. An Historical and Biographical Account of the Violin, with facsimiles of the labels of the Old Makers*. London: William Reeves, n.d.

Cozio di Salabue. *The Cozio Manuscripts*. Transcribed by Renzo Bachetta. Milan: Antonio Cardoni, 1950.

Doring, Ernest N. *How Many Strads?* Chicago: William Lewis & Son, 1945.

——. *The Guadagnini Family of Violin Makers.* Chicago: William Lewis & Son, 1949.

Doring, Ernest N., and Whistler, Harvey S. *Jean-Baptiste Villaume of Paris.* Chicago: William Lewis & Son, 1961.

Fairfield, John H. *Known Violin Makers.* New York: The Bradford Press, 1942.

Farga, Franz. *Violins and Violinists.* London: Rockliff, 1955.

Fleming, James M. *The Fiddle Fancier's Guide.* London: Haynes, Foucher & Co., 1892.

Hamma, Fridolin. *German Violin Makers.* London: William Reeves, 1961.

Hart, George. *The Violin: Its Famous Makers and Their Imitators.* London: Dulau and Co. and Schott and Co., 1875.

Haweis, H. R. *Old Violins and Violin Lore.* London: William Reeves, n.d. (reprint)

Henley, W. *Antonio Stradivari: Master Luthier, His Life and Instruments.* Brighton, England: Amati Publishing Co., Ltd., n.d.

Henry Hottinger Collection, The. New York: Rembert Wurlitzer, Inc., 1967.

Heron-Allen, Edward. *Violin-Making As It Was and Is.* London: Ward-Lock & Co., Ltd., n.d. (reprint)

Herrmann, Emil. *Two Masterpieces of Antonius Stradivarius (The King Maximilian 1709 and The Prinz Khevenhüller 1733).* New York: Emil Herrmann, n.d.

Hill, W. E. & Sons. *The Salabue Stradivari.* London: W. E. Hill & Sons, 1891.

Hill, W. Henry, Arthur F., and Alfred E. *Antonio Stradivari, His Life and Work (1644–1737).* London: W. E. Hill & Sons, 1902. Reprint. New York: Dover Publications, Inc. 1963.

——. *The Violin-Makers of the Guarneri Family (1626–1762).* London: W. E. Hill & Sons, 1931. Reprint. London: The Holland Press, Ltd., 1965.

Jalovec, Karel. *Encyclopedia of Violin Makers, 2 vols.* London: Paul Hamlyn, 1968.

——. *German and Austrian Violin Makers*. London: Paul Hamlyn, 1967.

——. *Italian Violin Makers*. rev. ed. London: Paul Hamlyn, 1964.

——. *The Violin Makers of Bohemia*. London: Anglo-Italian Publications, Ltd., 1965.

Loan Exhibition, Stringed Instruments and Bows. New York: Rembert Wurlitzer, Inc., 1966.

Lochner, Louis, *Fritz Kreisler*. New York: Macmillan, 1950.

Möller, Max. *The Violin-Makers of the Low Countries*. Amsterdam: Max Möller, 1955.

Mozart, Leopold. *A Treatise on the Fundamental Principles of Violin Playing*. London: Oxford University Press, 1967.

Narayn, Deane. *The Small Stradivari*. New York: Abelard-Schuman, Ltd., 1961.

Poidras, Henri. *Dictionary of Violin Makers*. Rouen: Imprimerie de la Vicomté, 1928.

Racster, Olga. *Chats on Violins*. London: T. Werner Laurie, 1905.

Reade, Charles. *Cremona Violins and Varnish*. New York: Alex. Broude, Inc., 1873. (reprint)

Retford, William C. *Bows and Bow Makers*. London: The Strad, 1964.

Roda, Joseph. *Bows for Musical Instruments of the Violin Family*. Chicago: William Lewis & Son, 1959.

Sandys, William, and Forster, Simon Andrew. *The History of the Violin*. London: William Reeves, 1864. (reprint)

Schebek, Dr. Edmund. *The Violin Manufacture in Italy and Its German Origin*. London: William Reeves, n.d.

Silverman, William Alexander. *The Violin Hunter, The Life Story of Luigi Tarisio, the Great Collector of Violins*. London: William Reeves, 1964.

Spohr, Louis. *Autobiography*. 1865. Reprint. New York: Da Capo Press, 1969.

Szigeti, Josef. *With Strings Attached*. New York: Alfred A. Knopf, 1966.

Tinyanova, Helen. *Stradivari the Violin-Maker*. New York: Alfred A. Knopf, 1938.

Van der Straeten, E. *The Romance of the Fiddle*. London: The London Press Company, 1911.

Vidal, Antoine. *La Lutherie et les Luthiers*. Paris, 1889. Reprint. Broude Bros., Ltd., 1969.

Wurlitzer, Rembert. *The Glory of Cremona*. Jacket notes for Decca Record DXSE7179, on which Ruggiero Ricci plays fifteen violins by famous makers ranging from Andrea Amati and Gasparo da Salò to Antonio Stradivari and Carlo Bergonzi.